MUSIC
OF A
THOUSAND
HAMMERS

MUSIC OF A THOUSAND HAMMERS

INSIDE HABITAT FOR HUMANITY

PAUL LEONARD

continuum

NEW YORK • LONDON

The Continuum International Publishing Group,
80 Maiden Lane, New York, NY 10038

The Continuum International Publishing Group Ltd,
The Tower Building, 11 York Road, London SE1 7NX

Cover art: University of Michigan Photo Services, Martin Vloet.

Cover design: Laurie Klein Westhafer

Library of Congress Cataloging-in-Publication Data

Leonard, Paul, 1940–
  Music of a thousand hammers : inside Habitat for Humanity / Paul Leonard.
    p. cm.
  Includes index.
  ISBN 0-8264-1842-2 (hardcover)
  1. Habitat for Humanity International, Inc. 2. Leonard, Paul, 1940–
  3. Low-income housing. I. Title.
  HV97.H32L46 2006
  363.5'83—dc22
                                    2006002319

Printed in the United States of America

06 07 08 09 10 11   10 9 8 7 6 5 4 3 2 1

To Judy, without whom there would be no music, and to Michael and Lilly Meyers, Ian and Sam Davis-Leonard, Paul and Scott Leonard, and Katy and Matthew Leonard, our grandchildren, in the hope that they too will hear music, if not of hammers, at least of other instruments of service to humanity.

Contents

Acknowledgments

I would have had little to write about without the wonderful experiences afforded by Habitat for Humanity over the past thirteen years. And I would not have made the effort to write without the encouragement and support of several friends and colleagues. My most vocal and faithful supporter has been my wife, Judy, who is also a worthy critic and stickler for details. Nic Retsinas, Habitat's current board chair, refers to this book as "Leonards Do Habitat," and he is exactly right.

During the time I was writing, Davidson College colleagues; John Kuykendall, Davidson's immediate past president; and Robert Henry Moore, a classmate and author in his own right, provided wise counsel and encouragement. I also am especially thankful for Jerry Shinn, a former associate editor of the *Charlotte Observer* and author of two recent books, for his editorial services and skill. Jerry provided insights on the book's organization and design as well.

I also want to express my deep appreciation to the Continuum International Publishing Group for its support and guidance with the book and, in particular, to Henry Carrigan, Amy Wagner, and Lauren Schneider who each contributed time, sound advice, and editing skills.

Our Towns Habitat volunteers will recognize some of the stories about people and places in that the stories first appeared in a column I wrote for *The Humanitarian*, the quarterly newsletter for Our Towns Habitat. Parts of the chapter on Houston were also quoted by Millard Fuller in his book, *More Than Houses*.

PROLOGUE
Hell Freezes Over

In November 2003, my wife, Judy, and I traveled to Auckland, New Zealand, to attend my final meeting of the board of directors of Habitat for Humanity International. I had served for eight years, the last two as chair, and the bylaws required that I rotate off the twenty-seven-member board in December.

Eight years earlier, neither Judy nor I could have fully appreciated the impact that serving on this board would have on our lives. We could not have anticipated the number of countries where we would help build Habitat homes, the blessings bestowed on us by Habitat families, and the joy of working with board members and volunteers from so many different places and cultures.

My departure from the board would not be the end of all that, of course. We knew our commitment to Habitat would remain strong and our work with the organization would continue to be a priority. But I assumed that my time in a leadership role with the organization was over, and I had already completed the first draft of this book about our experiences working around the world with Habitat. So I was completely surprised when, less than four months later, in mid March, my successor as chair, Rey Ramsey, telephoned me and said, "I may need you."

When I asked why, he told me the distressing news. A female employee at Habitat headquarters in Americus, Georgia, had accused

Habitat's founder and president, Millard Fuller, of sexual harassment. Rey said the board had retained a law firm to look into the charge.

Such an accusation would have seemed outrageous to almost anyone who knew much about Millard Fuller. He was a great man, a visionary, a person of mountain-moving faith, and his vision and faith had made believers over the years out of thousands of skeptics—including me. Surely one would not expect him to be guilty of any kind of sexual misconduct.

I knew that such an accusation is sometimes the result of a misunderstanding, a misinterpretation of an innocent gesture of affection. Perhaps that was the case now. Yet I also was aware that this was not the first time a female employee had accused Millard Fuller of inappropriate behavior. I knew there had been several incidents in the early 1990s, before I joined the board. During my term as chair, another woman claimed Millard had made inappropriate contact, making her uncomfortable. At that time we were able to resolve the matter with a discussion and follow-up letter in his employee file, warning him against doing anything a female employee might interpret as sexual harassment.

So it was clear to me that the board had to take this latest charge seriously. It also was clear that Habitat, which was sustained by volunteer labor and donor generosity, might have difficulty surviving under a chief executive whose reputation was tarnished by that kind of scandal.

I told Rey Ramsey I would do whatever he needed. And then I told Judy about my commitment to Rey. From that moment on Judy participated in every discussion with Rey. We both felt that if Habitat needed us, we had to respond.

Millard angrily denied the charges. The board instructed him not to talk with any of the employees being questioned by the outside investigator, but he ignored that order, and the board suspended him from the office until the investigation was complete. The board concluded that it was "likely" something had happened to cause the employee's complaint. Millard continued to deny the charges and insisted that he had been falsely accused. He asked former president Jimmy Carter, whose home is a few miles away in Plains and who had become Habitat's most visible and influential volunteer, to mediate his disagreement with the board. Despite President Carter's efforts, the situation continued to deteriorate.

The board suggested Millard undergo training and counseling on the subject of sexual harassment. He refused and said he was going to retire at the end of 2004. He would be seventy years old in January 2005. But since he would not agree to training or counseling, the board decided, for liability reasons, that it had to remove him from all day-to-day authority and control over employees.

Meanwhile, the executive committee of the board requested that I come to Americus and serve as managing director. Millard would continue in a speech-making and fund-raising role and as president and CEO, but I would be Habitat's managing director until a search committee could find a new CEO.

Some years earlier, Judy had told me hell would freeze over before she would ever move to Americus. I do not want our friends in Americus to misunderstand what she was saying. With a population of about seventeen thousand, it is a pleasant town full of good people, many of whom work for Habitat for Humanity. But it was a seven-hour drive from our home in Davidson, North Carolina. It was a very long distance, geographically and in other respects, from our leafy college town near a large lake and in the shadow of a vibrant city. Davidson and Charlotte were where our roots were and where most of our friends were, and six of our eight grandchildren lived within a fifteen-minute drive of our home there. So Judy did not want to move to Americus—or anywhere else.

But after more discussions with Rey Ramsey and other board members, Judy and I knew we would be moving to Americus sooner or later. We felt as though we were being called—and not just by Rey Ramsey.

Despite Judy's earlier comment about hell freezing over, there was never any question about what we should or would do. That would not surprise you if you knew Judy. I sometimes think of Judy when I hear Bette Midler sing about "the wind beneath my wings," but she is a lot more than wind under wings. She is strength alongside and often an engine in front. She is a born traveler, an unparalleled organizer, and the most faithful friend anyone could ever want. And she had been a believer in Habitat even before I was.

I met Judy in 1956 during my junior year of high school, when her family returned to Jonesboro, Georgia, from Louisiana. That fall we began dating, and by the following February we had decided to marry sometime in the future. It was the best decision I ever made, even though I was not old enough to make such decisions.

We waited as long as we could, until July 31, 1959, after my freshman year at Davidson. Judy's mother cried, and her father predicted that Judy would get pregnant right away and I would drop out of college and be a shipping clerk at Sears. Neither of those events occurred, and now, after forty-six years of marriage and raising four children, we know that we are the best friends either of us has ever had.

When our children were young, my management positions in the home-building industry required little travel. But as the children began to leave home, I started traveling extensively, first with Centex Homes, one of the nation's largest home builders, and then with Habitat for Humanity. And whenever possible, Judy was with me.

So that spring of 2004 we did not discuss whether I would move to Americus, or whether Judy would move with me. We talked instead about how we were going to handle the move and how it would change our lives. On June 13 we drove to Americus, and I began my new job the next day.

My arrival did not improve relations between Millard and the board, or between Millard and me. My differences with Millard regarding Habitat's current operations and future plans had surfaced most recently at my last board meeting in Auckland the previous November. After that meeting adjourned, the last words I heard from Millard on an issue of board governance were, "I don't want to talk about it anymore." Then, somewhat angry and hurt, he turned and walked away.

That unpleasant episode did not diminish the respect Millard and I had for each other. We continued to exchange letters and talk by phone. He was more than gracious in commenting to others about my board leadership. More than once during my board tenure, Millard reminded me that if two people always agreed, one of them was not thinking. From the beginning of my role as a board member, I accepted the responsibility to think carefully about Habitat's present and future and encouraged my colleagues on the board to do the same. If a founder and/or president has all the answers and with his staff can plan for the future and control the present, why have a board of directors? Isn't any board meant to be more than window dressing for donors?

The question at the center of most of my differences with Millard was whether Habitat for Humanity, as currently structured, staffed, and directed, with a presence in one hundred countries, had a chance of significantly addressing the mission of eliminating poverty housing from the world. Can it continue to rely mostly on inspiring speeches, prayer, direct mail appeals, independent affiliates, media events, a former president of the United States, and programs such as Building on Faith, Global Village, Women's Build, and others to sustain acceptable progress toward its goal? Can it, doing business as usual, consider itself to be a serious player in eliminating poverty housing from the face of the earth?

Out of a population of 6 billion, 1.3 billion people in urban areas and 2.6 billion people in rural areas live in substandard shelter. A billion people live in one-room shelters. One hundred million people are home-less. Ninety-five million housing units are needed every year just to shel-ter families moving into urban areas. For an organization dedicated to removing every shack and replacing it with a decent house, this should be sobering news. Our current claim to fame, completing a house some-where in the world every twenty-four minutes, will not get us to where the world needs us to go.

A week or so before I arrived in Americus, President Carter negoti-ated an agreement between Millard and the board. Millard would retire in January 2005 on his seventieth birthday but would continue to speak on behalf of Habitat and be involved in fund-raising and speaking. Habitat would continue to pay Millard and his wife, Linda, and provide health coverage as lifetime benefits. The agreement included a non-disparagement clause. My role was to serve as managing director until the board found and hired a new CEO. Meanwhile, Millard would not be involved in the management of Habitat.

The board and I hoped to avoid publicity about the charge against Millard. We wanted to keep the matter within the Habitat family, for Millard's sake and for the sake of the great organization he had created. But Millard's refusal to cooperate eventually made that impossible. His own and Linda's activities and statements quickly attracted the atten-tion of regional news media.

Millard signed the agreement in early June 2004, but it included a seven-day revocation period, as required by Georgia law. At the board meeting in Mexico City on June 10, Millard revoked the agreement and appealed to the board to reinstate him. The board voted to terminate him unless he honored the agreement. On June 16 the Fullers once again signed the agreement. But in the ensuing weeks, in violation of the agreement, they continued to lobby employees and supporters of Habi-tat, insisting that Millard had done nothing wrong and that the board was wrong to insist on his retirement.

The woman who had accused Millard of sexual harassment had agreed, after negotiations with the board, not to take legal action against him. But with the Fullers still fighting retirement and insisting on his innocence, it was not clear whether she would continue to honor that agreement.

I want to emphasize that Millard Fuller has not been tried and convicted for any wrongdoing. The board was not so much sitting in judgment of Millard as acting to protect the organization. Given the circumstances, it seems to me that the board's insistence that he relinquish day-to-day management was clearly in the best interests of Habitat and almost certainly in the best interests of Millard and Linda Fuller, and not at all unreasonable.

As the controversy continued, I worked to keep the headquarters operation focused on its tasks and to maintain morale on the staff. In mid summer, with no end to the conflict in sight, I drove ten miles to Plains to visit President Carter and ask for his advice. He urged me to try, despite Millard's refusal to cooperate, to maintain communications with Millard and keep him "in the loop," even as the board and I proceeded to do what we had to do. I told him I would try to do as he suggested.

Then he said, "I have a question for you."

I asked what it was.

"Are you going to see this through?" he asked.

"Yes, Mr. President," I said. "I will see it through."

As events subsequently unfolded, it became clear that President Carter had sensed the trouble ahead and wanted to know if I was committed and capable of facing it. There were numerous calls and letters of complaint about the board's eventual termination of Millard on January 31, 2005. One letter I received came from the director of urban ministries at a Presbyterian church in Los Angeles. Since I knew this person and her support of Habitat, I called her and then in a follow-up letter written in July 2005, explained the events at Habitat between April 2004 and July 2005 and my continued involvement.

My letter did not recite the chronology of events that occurred from April 2004 to Millard's termination on January 31, 2005. Its focus was more on what happened and why.

As with many decisions, it is usually one thing that triggers a decision, but it is generally not in itself the sole reason for that decision. Millard's relationship with the HFHI board had been deteriorating over a number of years and around a variety of issues; significant overruns on the Global Village and Discovery Center and total disregard by Millard for board resolutions regarding the same; Millard's lack of interest in succession planning or any other kind of planning; disagreement over low salaries and their impact on hiring competent staff; a focus on increasing

numbers of houses, affiliates, and countries and a disinterest in building
the organizational strength to control the same.

With this as background, the sexual harassment charge in the spring
of 2004 was just one more problem. The board's finding was that there
was insufficient proof of sexual harassment, not that there was no
proof, and its conclusion was that something likely happened, although
proof was uncertain. . . . It was never the board's intent to publicize any
of this, and it was the Fullers who brought public attention to the issue
through repeated conversations with the press, employees, and others.
The board bent over backwards to accommodate Millard's concerns,
one of which was to be present at the celebration of the 200,000th
house. The agreement signed by the Fullers in June 2004 and broken by
the Fullers the next month was renegotiated by President Carter again in
August and violated by the Fullers within a week. With my help a third
agreement was crafted in October 2004 just days before the board was
scheduled to meet and vote on Millard's termination. This agreement
required Millard to step aside as CEO while remaining as founder/
president for as long as he was physically able, i.e., no retirement date,
200,000th house celebration, speaking, fund-raising, etc. In early December Millard gave an interview to the Associated Press in which he
continued to attack the board and indirectly caused the name and location of his accuser to be released to the press. This act brought on a
threatened lawsuit from a case that had previously been settled and
ultimately led to Millard and Linda's termination on January 31, 2005.

In the end, the issue for the board was fire Millard or resign en
masse. Trust between the parties had dropped to zero, which is where it
remains today. President Carter noted on one occasion that Millard
broke both a solemn vow and a legal agreement. I do not fault the board
for its actions. In fact, it took extraordinary strength and commitment
to this ministry to act in the face of total defiance by its founder. While
all are saddened and troubled by the necessity of Millard's termination,
we believe that the ministry he and Linda founded is of God, and we
continue to pray, seek His guidance and will, and build houses for families in need.

The urban director had a second question that required an answer.
After Millard was fired, he formed a new organization, which he at
first named Building Habitat. Its purposes were identical to those of
Habitat, and he intended to raise funds and support Habitat affiliates
while bypassing the existing organization. When Rey Ramsey, the board

chair, and I heard of this, we immediately had our attorneys ask Millard to choose a different name. Millard refused, and Habitat sued him and his new organization. Her question was, why would Habitat be so unloving and mean toward its founder? The response . . .

> In regard to your question about our opposition to Millard's use of the name "Building Habitat," here is my position. Under Millard's watch Habitat challenged the Seventh-Day Adventists and a program they were launching called "Hope for Humanity." Habitat was able to resolve the issue short of a lawsuit. Under Millard's watch, Habitat challenged Dick Nojey for a program he launched called "Harvest for Humanity," and again Habitat resolved the issue without a lawsuit. There are several other examples where Habitat for a number of years has acted to protect its name.
>
> When Millard first filed the papers for Building Habitat, we put him on notice of what we regarded as a potential trademark infringement. He offered to provide some small-print disclosures to the effect that Building Habitat was not associated with Habitat for Humanity. We did not think this was sufficient. When I discussed the issue with President Carter, he remarked that only lawyers read the small print. Our attorneys met with Millard's attorney and offered to reimburse any costs he had incurred if they would drop the name Habitat. He refused. We filed suit.
>
> I agree with you that there are many organizations using the words *building* and *habitat*. But there is only one organization that has been incorporated with the same fund-raising purpose of Habitat for Humanity, by the same founder of Habitat for Humanity, and this is bound to lead to confusion in the minds of the public, our donors, and affiliates. It is obvious that Millard intends to use this vehicle to bypass Habitat for Humanity, which fired him, and to appeal to and directly support affiliates. It is a shrewd strategy on his part, but not one that those with fiduciary responsibility for Habitat for Humanity can let go by without challenging. If an organization does not act promptly to protect the name or trademark, anyone can begin to use it.
>
> In May 2005, a few days before a judge was to hear Habitat's complaint against Millard for trademark infringement, Millard agreed in a consent decree enforceable by the court to no longer trade in the name Building Habitat and to limit his references to Habitat for Humanity in his promotional materials. His stated reason for accepting the court decree was not to waste money on lawyers. I believe the real reason was

he was going to lose. His new organization is now called Fuller Center for Housing. Habitat continues to monitor his web site and promotional material to ensure that he is abiding by the consent decree.

The urban director's view that the feuding Habitat parties reconcile was not changed by my letter, and her view is reflective of a relatively small group of Millard's followers. For the most part, Habitat's affiliates, national organizations, individual donors, corporate sponsors, and staff have accepted the necessity of Millard's departure and are focused on the tremendous need for and future potential of Habitat.

I had told the board that during the transition period I would make changes necessary to position Habitat for the future. If they just wanted me to go to Americus and be a hand holder, they had the wrong man. It was extremely difficult to make any serious progress in changing Habitat's focus while Millard was still on the scene. In spite of his role having been limited by the board to speaking and fund-raising events, Millard continued to interact with staff and control those whom he could. And there had been the constant news about the conflict between the board and the founder.

I began work in Americus on June 14, 2004. I had reached out to Millard over the previous weekend, and we had lunch together early in that first week. During lunch, Millard professed his innocence, disparaged his accuser, attacked specific board members, and faulted the investigative process. My strategy in the beginning was to listen not only to Millard but to as many of our employees as I could.

At that time Habitat employed more than four hundred people in Americus and close to one thousand worldwide. My administrative assistant scheduled department meetings so that I could introduce myself to each department and answer any questions employees might have about Habitat, the changes that were under way, and the future. Immediately following the department meetings, she scheduled individual times for me to stop by each office and cubicle to meet with employees one-on-one. I would introduce myself and ask about their work with Habitat, how long they had been with us, what was motivating about their work, and what was frustrating. They asked questions as well.

Nothing else I did in the following fifteen months had the impact of these one-on-one meetings, and nothing else I accomplished would have been possible without the goodwill and trust this simple activity generated. Time after time employees said Habitat management had not done this before. In other words, our managers had not taken the time to thank and listen to each employee on an individual basis. It was a wonderful learning experience and a chance to garner a deep appreciation for the commitment these employees have to the mission of Habitat. I also let them know they could talk to me anytime.

In October 2004 we started changing the organizational structure. It was clear that the functional departments housed in Americus—including communications, finance, human resources, resource development, legal, and information services—were not working together and furthermore were not providing acceptable service to the rest of the organization. The existing organizational structure had included Millard as founder, president, and CEO, with a COO (chief operating officer) reporting to him. All other department heads worked for the COO.

After trying to work through the COO, it was apparent that the only way to influence the culture and change attitudes was to eliminate the COO position and have the department leaders report directly to me. While I offered the COO a newly created position as executive vice president for USA/Canada, he began his own job search and left Habitat. The senior vice president of resource development also left Habitat. He had been close to Millard and felt this would hurt his future with Habitat.

From October 2004 to August 2005, six other department heads resigned. In every case because of either burnout or personality, it seemed best both for the individual and for Habitat that these changes occur. But you can image the turmoil such changes create. Thoughtfully, Judy supplied my office with a box of Kleenex, which got plenty of use. With the help of my staff, we have been able to fill three of the vacated positions and searches are under way for the others. To Habitat's benefit, all of our international program vice presidents have remained in place and kept us focused on our housing mission, whether in Budapest, Bangkok, Johannesburg, or San Jose.

One telling example of what our new corporate structure and spirit of cooperation have produced is Habitat's tsunami relief project. When the Asian tsunami hit on December 26, 2004, Steve Weir, our area vice president for Asia Pacific, was vacationing with his wife in Sri Lanka. We lost communication with Steve for a few days, but when we connected, Steve was focused on the disaster and Habitat's role. What followed then was a series of nightly telephone calls between Steve and the international executive vice president and representatives of our finance, human resources, and communications departments. Habitat had six affiliates in Sri Lanka that were in the path of the tsunami and several other operations on the east coast of India and in Thailand and Indonesia. Because of the scale of the disaster, it took weeks to assess the impact and damage.

Steve knew, however, that we could not just focus on the twenty-six hundred Habitat homeowners in Sri Lanka, some of whose homes had been lost or damaged, or the twenty-seven hundred families then working toward a new Habitat house. We needed a bolder and more dynamic approach. Our nightly telephone team proposed with Steve's inspiration that we commit to build or restore twenty-five thousand homes in the tsunami-impacted areas in two years and projected that Habitat would have to raise $25 million to achieve this goal.

Because we now had all of our departments working together, communicating, and cooperating, in three months Habitat launched a campaign and raised over $50 million with plans to build and/or restore thirty-five thousand homes. Throughout Habitat's history, at least 92 percent of all funds raised came from the United States. For the tsunami, funds pledged from Asia and Europe equaled those pledges from the United States! Provided Habitat proves itself capable of executing this relief program and faithfully reports to its donors, an entirely new window of support and opportunity has been opened for this global ministry.

The tsunami reminded all of us that the need for housing in this world far outstrips the resources on hand to help. It refocused Habitat and its staff on its mission and put the issues with Millard in the rear window. In August 2005, Habitat dedicated its 200,000th house in Knoxville, Tennessee. It took Habitat and its affiliates twenty-five years to build the first one hundred thousand houses, and the next one hundred thousand were completed in just less than five years. When we dedicated the house in Knoxville, we also recognized that one million people have been served by Habitat. But just so we didn't let this wonderful occasion distort our vision, we built the 200,001st house in India and dedicated it twenty-four minutes after the Knoxville dedication. Our theme was "Much to Celebrate, More to Build." The house built and dedicated on India's east coast where the tsunami hit reminds us of the houses still needed in the world. The tsunami destroyed 200,000 houses in minutes.

As I leave Habitat and turn over the reins to our new CEO, Jonathan Reckford, I am entrusting him with a draft of a new five-year strategic plan that the board and staff have created over the last five months. The intent of this plan is to grow the ministry exponentially through partnerships with others, increased focus on access to capital, and a strengthening of the organization's competency in all departments and functions. The plan is supported by clearly articulated initiatives and business case analyses. Most importantly, the plan recognizes that Habitat must work with other non-governmental organizations and governments to address the issues of poverty and to transform communities.

Jonathan is also inheriting a U.S. operation that has been reorganized and refocused. There are approximately 1,670 U.S. Habitat affiliates building, repairing, or rehabilitating 5,000 houses per year. The majority of these affiliates are building one or two houses annually. For Habitat to grow, it must lend energy and support to the affiliates that are interested in growing and capable of raising the resources to support that growth. Our new organizational structure encourages this to happen.

Habitat will have a national call center to provide basic support for information, forms, manuals, reports, and so on for all affiliates and a support staff to focus on the affiliates that want more guidance and that will enter into consulting agreements detailing the improvements sought. We will focus more intently on the urban affiliates that face issues of high land costs, multi-family structures, and neighborhood associations. As a result of these changes, we expect to increase the number of houses Habitat is building in the United States and to see our affiliates play a larger role in the housing and community issues in their towns and cities.

Six days before Jonathan Reckford became Habitat's CEO, Hurricane Katrina devastated areas in Latin America and the Gulf States of Alabama, Mississippi, and Louisiana. Under Jonathan's leadership Habitat faced the aftermath of Katrina head-on with the creation of its Operation Home Delivery. In the fall of 2005 Operation Home Delivery captured the hearts and good will of many Americans as thousands of volunteers began to build containerized house frames we called "House-in-a-Box." NBC's Today Show transformed Rockefeller Plaza into Humanity Plaza and built forty-five house frames in five days working 24/7. Freddie Mac built fifty-one house frames in ten days on the National Mall in Washington, D.C., at Thanksgiving. Habitat was the single charity supported by the televised Emmy Awards in Los Angeles and eight house frames were built during the 2005 baseball World Series.

These efforts generated over $70 million for the victims of Katrina and enabled Habitat's Hurricane Katrina Task Force to plan for the building of thousands of new homes in the Gulf States over the next several years.

A new and talented CEO, vibrant programs to restore communities impacted by the Asian tsunami of 2004 and Hurricane Katrina in 2005, a new five-year strategic plan, and a reorganized and focused U.S. operation are all strong signals that Habitat has emerged from the crisis with its founder stronger, better focused and equipped to build houses and transform communities around the world.

In some ways it will not be easy to leave this exciting work and return to my home in Davidson, North Carolina. Judy and I will miss the Habitat staff and board that have faithfully supported us and courageously coped with the changes and uncertainties of the last eighteen months. I will never forget the four employees who appeared at my office after devotions one morning at 8:00 and asked if they could pray for me and Judy. I not only welcomed their prayers; I needed them. At the conclusion of that morning's prayer, they told me they were my "prayer warriors." And prayer warriors they were, showing up each morning thereafter to hold hands and pray for me, Judy, and Habitat. Nor will I forget the many thank-yous from staff in Americus and around the world, from affiliate executive directors, and from others who appreciated our presence in the midst of the turmoil.

I will remember forever the unfailing support of President Carter. He was always just a telephone call away, accessible and supportive. In one meeting with him at the Carter Center in Atlanta months after Millard's termination, I asked if he remembered the question he had asked me when we first met in Plains in June 2004. He said that he did and that my answer that day also convinced him to see it through. With the help, support, and prayers of many, including President Carter, my hope is that we have not only preserved Habitat but positioned it for an even more dynamic future with new leadership and a larger vision.

Davidson, North Carolina
February 2006

PART 1
EPIPHANY

1

BEFORE HABITAT

Judy and I both had a life before Habitat for Humanity, but we have difficulty remembering it. A few years ago we were walking in our neighborhood early one morning. At that time, Judy chaired the Family Selection Committee and served on the board of Charlotte Habitat. I was president of Our Towns Habitat in Davidson, North Carolina, and treasurer of the board of directors of Habitat for Humanity International. Judy was sharing her frustration with a family issue in Charlotte, and I was telling her about the serious need for an operating reserve for Habitat's international operations. Suddenly I stopped and looked at Judy and asked, "Don't we have anything to talk about but Habitat?"

"We need to get a life!" she said.

We both laughed and resumed our walk talking about you-know-what.

It's hard to believe now that I turned down my first opportunity to volunteer with Habitat in 1986. I was president of the John Crosland Company in Charlotte. Crosland was the largest privately owned home builder in the Southeast, with operations in Charlotte and Raleigh in North Carolina; Charleston, Myrtle Beach, and Columbia in South Carolina; and Atlanta, Georgia. Overseeing these operations demanded a lot of my time, but that was not the reason I first passed up the chance to work with Habitat for Humanity.

I am not sure when my working career began. That would depend on how you defined it. I worked weekends at my brother-in-law's gas station at twelve. I ran a truck stop on U.S. Highway 41 just south of Atlanta the summer I was fourteen, working twelve-hour days. Between the ages of fourteen and eighteen, I bagged groceries, worked as a mason tender, scooped ice cream, drove a supply truck for a steel erection company, and worked for the Plant Pest Control Division of the U.S. Department of Agriculture in Atlanta. These were all part-time and/or summer jobs during my high school years. Out of my earnings I paid $10 per week in rent to my dad and stepmother.

Somewhere in the midst of all this activity, I managed to finish at the top of my high school class, decided I was called to the ministry, and found and fell in love with Judy Moore. Despite the costs of cars and dating, I saved $600 for college. With $100 from my dad, another $600 from my local church, and a Staley Memorial Scholarship, I enrolled as a freshman at Davidson College, part of the class of 1962, as a pre-ministerial student. The following summer Judy and I married, and she joined me at Davidson, working while I went to school. I worked as a supply preacher on Sundays and in the summers went back to the USDA's Plant Pest Control Division.

Maybe you are wondering how a pre-ministerial student ended up as president of a home-building company. So have I. Even as I recall the journey, I still wonder.

During my last three years at Davidson, I preached at three rural congregations. Judy and I lived in a mobile home two miles from town with a garden and a dog named Pepper.

After graduating from Davidson with a degree in history and a minor in philosophy, I enrolled at the Divinity School of the University of Chicago in the fall of 1962. Judy and I looked like the Beverly Hillbillies driving our black 1957 Volkswagen and her dad's blue Chevrolet pickup with its wooden sides and all our belongings up the highway, out of the familiar South and into the unknown Midwest. We felt like space aliens from a rural planet when we arrived at 5482 Greenwood Avenue, in urban Chicago.

At the Divinity School I learned, among other things, about the suburban captivity of the church, from Gibson Winter, my professor in sociology and religion. After I completed my academic degree work at the end of my second year, Judy and I spent an intern year in the captivity of one of those suburban churches—Trinity Presbyterian, in Charlotte—working with children and youth under the direction of the Christian education committee. I accepted Trinity's invitation to become its associate minister at the conclusion of my intern year and never returned to the University of Chicago, graduating in absentia on June 11, 1965.

Strange as it may seem, Trinity got me into housing, at least indirectly. Trinity created the opportunity for me to meet and hear Gwen Heard. She was a Mecklenburg County home demonstration agent in Charlotte, who came to Trinity one Tuesday morning in 1966 to speak to a women's group about her work. That's when I heard her tell a story that changed my life—the story of the Anthony family.

When Ms. Heard met the Anthonys, they had just arrived in Charlotte from South Carolina and were living in a small house with Mr. Anthony's brother and his family. Through Ms. Heard, the Anthonys found an apartment in Earle Village public housing. That seemed to me a worthy accomplishment until she showed pictures of the double bed on which four children slept crosswise and told us about the second-hand furniture store that charged Mr. Anthony $150 for a 1938 Norge washing machine.

The story has stayed with me for thirty-eight years. It broke my heart and at the same time kindled my determination. I became involved in a fair housing movement and was the first president of the Charlotte Fair Housing Association. Our mission was to prevent discrimination in the sale and rental of housing in the Queen City. Volunteers shopped for houses and apartments after families were denied access based on race.

Our efforts were not universally applauded. I once spent a night in the home of an African-American family that had just moved into a previously all-white neighborhood. Someone had fired shots into the house during their first night there. Judy and I received threatening calls at home and talked about moving our children out of the front bedrooms, fearing for their safety.

After three years, I left Trinity to accept a three-year grant from the United Presbyterian Church to organize an experimental congregation in Charlotte. The new church was to focus, not on building bigger and better facilities for itself, but on community needs, which is why it was considered experimental. It would still be experimental today. I trust that God forgives the ironies perpetuated in his name.

Our new Church in the City leased a house for its worship, office, and meetings and founded and operated a nonprofit day-care center for fifty inner-city children. It also organized a nonprofit housing corporation,

Urban Homes, Inc., in partnership with the congregations of the Charlotte Friends Meeting and the Little Rock AME Zion Church. With just
$1,200 contributed by the three congregations, the corporation man-
aged to develop a twenty-two-lot subdivision called Clawson Village,
on Little Hope Road in South Charlotte, and build twenty-two houses
there for low-income families. As president of Urban Homes, I learned
about site development, zoning, subdivision ordinances, construction,
and loan approvals for families.

It was a total surprise, and one of those marvelous coincidences that
God is always arranging, when the Anthonys became the first family to
apply for and move into a home in Clawson Village.

Something about building houses and giving concrete hope to people
touched a need deep within me. I heard someone remark recently that
there is no need walking somewhere to preach unless in your walking
you are living the sermon. Safe, decent, affordable homes for low-
income families was a walk I wanted to take.

I then joined a new city nonprofit housing corporation, Motion,
Inc., and planned to continue as minister of Church in the City. Five
months into my new job, I realized I had to choose between the formal
ministry for which I had prepared and an informal ministry that built
houses for people in need. With Judy's support, I chose home building.

As Motion's associate director and later executive director, I helped
develop a scattered-site single-family program that utilized modular
houses and two inner-city apartment communities built in partnership
with a private developer, the John Crosland Company.

Motion sent me to the Housing Specialists Institute in Washington,
D.C., for six weeks to gain knowledge of apartment development equivalent to the knowledge I had gained of single-family development by
trial and error with Clawson Village and Urban Homes.

Careers are unpredictable. You never know when a future you
thought was secure is suddenly beyond your control. In January 1973
President Nixon declared a moratorium on all federal housing programs, specifically Sections 235 and 236 of the National Housing Act.
These programs either provided a subsidy for qualified families that
reduced their mortgage payments to the equivalent of a 1 percent interest rate or made rents available on a similar basis. They were the very
programs on which Motion depended. Without those subsidies Motion
had little future.

President Nixon's order was not retroactive. Projects in the planning
pipeline could still be developed. Motion was working on two apartment

projects with the John Crosland Company. In May, during a meeting with Herman Alley, a Crosland vice president, he asked if I might be interested in working in his company's Apartment Division. Crosland was looking for someone to help administer its multi-family projects, find sites, secure investors, and work with the Department of Housing and Urban Development on loan processing and inspections. Knowing that Motion could not survive the loss of the federal subsidies, and knowing of Crosland's commitment to affordable housing, I told Herman I was interested.

After completing an application and taking a series of tests, I had a ninety-minute interview with John Crosland. A few days later Crosland extended a job offer, which I accepted. Thus began a fourteen-year career with the John Crosland Company that included a promotion to company president in 1984.

In the early years with Crosland, I had the opportunity to oversee the development, construction, and/or rehabilitation of more than eighteen hundred housing units for low-income families. We developed many more houses and apartments for middle-income families.

This is not a story about my work with Crosland or subsequently with Centex Homes, which purchased Crosland's home-building operations in 1987. It is a story about my volunteer time with Habitat for Humanity. But perhaps this background will help explain why my first response to the invitation to join Habitat was, "No, thank you."

Using government funds and tax deferments, borrowing as much as possible, paying interest, making a profit, and employing professional builders, through Crosland I was helping to complete three hundred to four hundred units of affordable housing each year. Certainly there was a tremendous need for such housing then, even as there is today. So along came Habitat for Humanity, launching a program in Charlotte to build one house at a time with donated money, charging no interest, adding no profit, and depending on the labor of volunteers and the intended homeowners. My reaction: Do that if you like. I certainly won't stand in your way. Maybe it will make you feel good. But you are kidding yourself if you think it will have any significant impact.

"No, thank you."

Maybe my years in the private sector, my belief in numbers and dollars, my experience with the sometimes harsh realities of the marketplace, invaluable as they were to all that I wanted to accomplish, had narrowed my vision. Maybe all that had dulled my idealism, even to some extent eroded the faith that had led me to the ministry as a younger man. Whatever the reason, I never would have believed what I now know: that by its thirtieth anniversary in 2006, Habitat for Humanity will have completed over two hundred thousand homes housing a million people in one hundred countries.

What had I failed to see?

2

SECOND CHANCE

We don't always get a second chance in life. But God is good, and sometimes we do. In this case, thank God, I did.

Another reason I had plenty to do in 1986 when Habitat came calling was that the John Crosland Company was for sale. With its success and sales volume increasing from $30 million to $75 million to $105 million in a three-year period, Crosland had outrun its capital. For growth to continue, the company required more capital. After an eighteen-month process of discussion, research, and exploration, enduring visits and interviews with ten companies, Crosland chose to sell its home-building operations to Centex Real Estate Corporation, a publicly traded home builder based in Dallas, Texas. Centex told us from our first meeting that they were interested in land and people and that they would run their own numbers, laying aside Crosland's carefully prepared five-year history of operations and future projections. I was one of the people Centex kept, and on October 1, 1987, I gave up my suit and tie for slacks and a polo shirt and became an executive vice president of Centex Real Estate Corporation.

One of the things that did not interest Centex was affordable housing—at least not any that was subsidized and available for low-income families. Whereas the focus at Crosland had been on marketing, customer satisfaction and community involvement, the focus at Centex was on cost control, predictability, and increasing margins. In my new role with Centex, I managed most of the old Crosland operations, which under Centex became full-fledged operating units with presidents and controllers. I also added an existing Centex Division in Nashville, Tennessee, and started a new one in Virginia Beach, Virginia. Like other executive vice presidents with Centex, I took on national responsibility for certain areas of training—land development, financial management, and leadership. This added duty required extensive national travel and conferences. But except for the blessing a new home brings to all families fortunate enough to own one, I could no longer argue that my work benefited families like the Anthonys, with the greatest housing needs.

Meanwhile, Habitat for Humanity, with former president Jimmy Carter's support, had become a well-known nonprofit builder and was ranked among the top one hundred builders in the nation. In the fall of 1991, I received a call from Bob Wilson, who owns ROWBOAT Dock & Dredge in Mooresville, North Carolina. Bob had organized and run several Jimmy Carter Work Projects for Habitat, and had agreed to organize a 1992 project in Washington, D.C. He knew of my work with Crosland and Centex and wanted to talk to Centex about a new program and partnership Habitat for Humanity International was beginning with the National Association of Home Builders (NAHB). It was called Homes Across America and was intended to encourage local home builders to join local Habitat affiliates in building homes for families. Centex was one of the five largest home builders in the United States at that time, and Bob thought that if he could get us to commit to the program, many others would follow. I told him the next time Tim Eller, then president of Centex Homes, was in town, I would set up a meeting.

Some weeks later Tim and I had lunch with Bob at a McDonald's in Cornelius, North Carolina. Bob asked Tim if Centex would consider building twenty homes with Habitat in 1992, which would have been a $1 million commitment. In return, Centex would be recognized as a sponsor of one of the houses in the Jimmy Carter Work Project in Washington. Tim listened and asked about participation by subcontractors and suppliers. After the meeting, Tim wanted my opinion. I told him Bob's request was worth considering because it would give Centex an opportunity to give back to its communities, and we would get favorable publicity because of the Washington event. Otherwise, I did not try to sell Tim on the Habitat proposal or argue that it was the right thing to do. Nevertheless, I thought it would benefit the company.

A few weeks later, somewhat to my surprise, Tim called and said, "Tell Bob Centex will build the twenty houses, including one in the Jimmy Carter Work Project in Washington. And by the way, Paul, you are in charge of coordinating with Habitat." Please note that Tim did not ask me if I wanted this new assignment added to my other responsibilities. He told me. He also did not mandate anyone else's cooperation. He simply gave permission for the company to work with Habitat. At the time, Centex was building in forty cities around the United States. It would be up to me to persuade twenty of those division presidents to participate in the Habitat project. I did not feel particularly grateful at the time, but I should have. Tim Eller had given me a second chance to "volunteer" with Habitat.

Judy and I spent five days with several Centex officers and Washington-area employees, other volunteers, and a Habitat family, building a home. That was when I finally understood the meaning, purpose, and power of Habitat. I had been right, of course: Habitat's approach was not the most efficient way to build an affordable house. But it was and is the best and most powerful way to build dignity for its families and to create community by bridging the social and economic divide that cuts across our world. At the Jimmy Carter Work Project in Washington, D.C., and at every Habitat for Humanity house-building project, you check your title, status, wallet, pedigree, color, gender, education, and background at the door. You then work on common ground. You quickly discover what people of goodwill can accomplish together. You understand, maybe for the first time in your life, the pure joy a house brings to a family desperate for a simple, decent, safe place to live. You see that joy in the smile of the parents and in the excitement of their children. And you know, without a doubt, that in this work you yourself have been blessed most of all. That's what I had failed to see in 1986. Habitat for Humanity does more than build houses.

Just so that this broader truth about Habitat for Humanity's work was not lost on me, two other opportunities to work on Habitat houses presented themselves in the summer and fall of 1992. The Charlotte Division of Centex Homes chose to participate in the Homes Across America program, and Judy and I joined their staff on their Habitat workday. Then Trinity Presbyterian Church, to which Judy and I had returned as members, decided to build a house. We both worked on that project. In each of those three 1992 Habitat work experiences, the excitement of working on common ground with others, the joy and smiles of the Habitat families, and the sense of a blessing received turned my reasoned "No, thank you" into a passionate "Yes—every chance I get."

The Habitat experience seemed to have a similar impact on Centex Homes. Reports coming from divisions working with Habitat spoke in glowing terms of the satisfaction and joy their staffs had on Habitat workdays. The construction superintendents loved seeing the sales teams work on siding. There was also a sense of pride that their company was helping the community, and everyone was caught up in the joy of the Habitat families. Building with Habitat became an annual tradition among Centex divisions, and the twenty houses in 1992 turned into between fifteen and twenty Habitat homes a year for the next five years, a gift approaching $5 million. Then in 1998 Centex announced another commitment to Habitat for Humanity of twenty houses a year for five more years.

In regard to Habitat, my wife, Judy, was a lot smarter than I was. She initially became involved with Habitat in 1990 as part of a community course in leadership. At first, Judy would volunteer in the office of Charlotte Habitat, working on their database. Then she joined our church's siding crew and became a regular construction volunteer. We didn't talk about Habitat much in those days, because I had thought since 1986 that Habitat wouldn't be very effective. And besides, I was too busy.

3

FAST FORWARD

After the excitement, challenge, and joy of our 1992 Habitat work experiences, Judy and I volunteered for the July 1993 Jimmy Carter Work Project in Winnipeg, Canada. We traveled to Winnipeg with other volunteers from Charlotte Habitat. There in five days we completed a house with a native North American family and deepened our friendship with and respect for our fellow travelers. There is nothing like the challenge of building a house in five days to test the mettle of a group, to discover how fast and hard you can work, to see how you react to the frustration of correcting mistakes, to test your persistence as the sun sets on your tired body and there is still work to do.

Two memories linger from Winnipeg. The first is of the shaman, or holy man, who participated in the house dedication and blessed the house by driving the evil spirits from the corners of each room. I subsequently have participated in house dedications for Buddhist and Muslim families. Each of these events reveals Habitat's commitment to love, serve, and build for all peoples and faiths openly, with no religious coercion or requirements.

The second memory is of our morning devotions and the music provided by Steve Bell. I still listen to his tapes. At midweek as our energy and spirits were sagging, Steve sang "Wings of an Eagle," based on Isaiah 40:31. The hopeful refrain running through Steve's song was,

"On the wings of an eagle, we will rise." The New Revised Standard Version expresses the message this way: "Those who wait for the LORD shall renew their strength, they shall mount up with wings like eagles, they shall run and not be weary, they shall walk and not faint."

Now when my spirit falters, I read Isaiah 40 or listen to Steve's song. The spirit of this song lifts me up every time. And then I remember other devotions from other Habitat builds and experiences that filled my heart and let me know that God had touched that person, changed his life, rescued her when she was falling, held them when they were hurting. And I give thanks that a Habitat workday begins in prayer.

A year after Winnipeg, Judy and I went to the Jimmy Carter Work Project in Eagle Butte, South Dakota. There the challenge was to build thirty-four homes and an $80,000 play structure donated by Owens Corning on a Lakota Reservation, and to do it all in five days. Arriving at midnight on Saturday, we were issued a pup tent and two cots and sent to the school playground in search of our tent site. We awoke Sunday morning in a tent city housing some fifteen hundred volunteers, including Jimmy and Rosalynn Carter in a traditional tepee.

Sunday was a day of parades and celebration led by the Lakota people. We walked through the town and rode to the site where work would begin on Monday. I was disappointed to discover that I was assigned to work on the play structure and not a house. It was a disappointment that quickly lifted as I joined the playground crew and discovered that I would be working with the children of our Habitat families.

Eagle Butte shows the length to which Habitat will go to demonstrate its belief that every person deserves a simple, decent place to sleep at night. Sleeping under the stars there, it was obvious that we were a long way from any city—no Wal-Mart, no Kmart, no Ace Hardware, no electrical supply house, no lumberyard, and no paint store. It was a logistical nightmare that Centex never would have attempted. Habitat's lead team worked for a year counting and ordering framing lumber, windows, doors, roof trusses, felt, roof shingles, siding, flooring, appliances, hardware, plumbing and electrical supplies, and other materials.

I do not know if you have ever heard the music of a thousand hammers. But Monday morning in Eagle Butte, there was a symphony, a cacophony of sound that reached the heavens and must have pleased the Father of all who labored in love and sweat below. That is what I like about the first morning of a blitz in North America: the sound of hammers, hammering out equity, hammering out love, hammering out hope and the excitement of walls being raised and houses rising with the morning sun. This is grassroots Habitat. There is where all the planning, talking, fretting, and fund-raising fade, and what is real and tangible takes form.

Yet the sound of Habitat in North America is different from its sound in Guatemala or Ghana, where we build with cement blocks or mud bricks. There you hear the symphony of children singing; workers laughing; trowels being scraped across blocks; and sand, cement, and water being mixed on the ground and poured into trenches. The Father hears this sound too, and he is pleased, knowing that his will is being done.

The sun, wind, and rain of the South Dakota plains in July welcomed us with a full display of their awesome power. We faced the four directions during the morning devotion, paying our respect and seeking the blessing of mother earth and father sky. Days one and two went well with the usual competition and the "borrowing" of materials that transpires among crews determined to finish before the others. Then we discovered that the siding materials on site were 50 percent short, a sure threat to our goal of completing all thirty-four houses by Friday.

Sometime Wednesday Habitat's desperate order reached the distributor in Texas, and a tractor trailer was loaded with a shipping ticket addressed to Habitat's headquarters in Americus, Georgia, some two thousand miles southeast of Eagle Butte. Before our blessed driver crossed the Mississippi River, he took another look at the shipping ticket and turned toward Eagle Butte. No load he ever carried was met with more enthusiasm and excitement than this. When he arrived early Friday morning, volunteers and house leaders looking for siding besieged truck and driver.

The material shortfall wasn't the only challenge at Eagle Butte. Habitat homeowners must have a steady source of income, because they are required to repay their mortgages on a monthly basis for twenty years. Life and income on a rural reservation such as Eagle Butte are tenuous at best, and after the Jimmy Carter Work Project left town, staff stayed for months to boost the local Habitat effort and to find ways these families could keep their homes. Carefully selecting Habitat families is a difficult task for the best affiliates. Doing this under the pressure of a week's build or blitz is an unbelievable burden and one that can burn out the local volunteers.

On Friday night we celebrated the completion of the thirty-four homes and thanked God and each other in a service of song, prayer, and speeches by Millard Fuller and Jimmy Carter. The next day we broke camp and headed west to Seattle to visit family. Given the opportunity to purchase our tent and cots for a nominal sum, Judy and I became the proud owners of our Eagle Butte estate. If you come for a visit, you might find yourself on one of those cots. We keep the tent for special sleep-outs with the grandchildren. And we'll keep Eagle Butte in our minds and hearts forever.

Jimmy Carter Work Projects like Winnipeg and Eagle Butte are wonderful and moving examples of the spirit of Habitat at work. They fast-forward Habitat's mission by generating excitement among volunteers and the general public as well. Yet most Habitat houses are built by our local affiliates where the pace is slower, the excitement level is significantly lower, and the challenge is to sustain the effort, week after week and year after year, supported mostly by volunteers. In 1994 I began to understand this truth.

4

GRASS ROOTS

A few months before we went to Winnipeg, Judy and I sold our home in Charlotte, moved into an apartment, and began construction of a new home on Lake Norman near Mooresville, North Carolina. When we sold our house that May, Judy was in Tucson, Arizona, with some friends and our daughter Rachel. It was my task in Charlotte to find and lease a three-bedroom apartment. Since much of my career involved planning, building, and managing apartment communities, this should have been an easy task for me, and it was—but I did not notice the building's six air-conditioning units outside the master bedroom window. Living in that apartment for six months tested both our marriage and our sanity. It also made me question why I had even developed apartments in the first place.

In November, as the new house was nearing completion, I was in Nashville with Martin Kerr, the Nashville Division president for Centex Homes. His mobile phone rang, and he answered it and then handed it to me. Judy was on the phone crying and complaining because Martin's counterpart in Centex's Charlotte Division, Randy Luther, had added one more week to our move-in date. I told Martin I had an irate homeowner on the phone. We both laughed before I called Randy to tell him the Leonards needed to move as scheduled—please, just finish the house!

The Lake Norman residence was to be our retirement house. My long-term goal was to retire at age fifty-five, just fourteen months away. Our new home also gave us a chance to reacquaint ourselves with the small towns of northern Mecklenburg and southern Iredell counties—Huntersville, Cornelius, Davidson, and Mooresville. I say reacquainted because thirty-one years earlier Judy and I had lived in Davidson while I attended college. It also gave us a chance to volunteer on Saturdays with Our Towns Habitat, which served those four towns.

One Saturday morning, Judy and I went to East McLelland Street in Mooresville, where Our Towns Habitat was framing a house. We worked with the "Over-the-Hill Gang" led by Henry Eddy, the father of Habitat in Mooresville. Because Judy and I had developed a few construction skills, Judy on the church's siding crew and I at Carter Work Projects, Henry asked for our names as we left work that day. He mentioned that the gang would be rehabilitating a house in Davidson the next week and asked us to come. Since I had not yet retired, Judy went by herself and amazed the crew with her ability to install soffit and talk at the same time.

More than any other person, Henry Eddy is responsible for cementing my relationship with Habitat. Since his retirement from the plumbing wholesale business more than seventeen years ago, Henry has had a laser focus on Habitat for Humanity. Of the one hundred houses built by Our Towns Habitat since 1989, Henry has worked on at least ninety. Neither kidney cancer nor a knee replacement has deterred him. He says that the house dedications are his paydays when he sees the smiles, hugs the children, and sings "Amazing Grace" one more time.

There are Henry Eddys in almost every thriving Habitat affiliate in the United States. In Portland's West Willamette affiliate, it's Al Vance; in Jackson, Mississippi, Elise Winter; in Charlotte, Hal Cole and Gene Davant.

After I had worked on his crew for several Saturdays, Henry pulled me aside and asked, "Will you be a house leader for us?"

My hands-on construction experience comes from Habitat. My roles at Crosland and Centex were more management and finance driven. But I had spent many hours at those companies inspecting projects, asking questions, and observing the processes, from foundation to final trim. Henry was Our Towns' only house leader, and he needed help. I could not turn him down. So I accepted with this condition: "Let's co-lead the next house first, and you teach me the tricks."

One of the tricks Henry had already taught me was not to be the volunteer who blows the insulation in the attic in the middle of a Carolina summer.

Before many months passed Henry and I had co-led and completed a house for Crystal Forney and her children, and I was on my own leading house number ten on McLelland Avenue with Debra Patrick and her teenage son and daughter. When Debra's friends asked her how she got her new house, she told them, "I earned it!" Her response helped me understand the pride that sweat equity can instill in a homeowner.

One thing I learned quickly as a house leader was to be sure to have crew leaders on site who know the craft or trade needed at the moment. I was not embarrassed at all to call on the petite Jane Cain, the organist at the Davidson College Presbyterian Church, to lead the roofing crew. Jane can tickle the ivories, but she also knows how to roof a house, and she loves it.

I was enjoying my role as volunteer house leader when Henry nominated me for the board of directors of Our Towns Habitat in mid 1995. Habitat's strength is at the grass roots, where volunteers in over 1,670 cities and towns take the ideas and principles of Habitat and apply them in their own communities. Habitat requires local entrepreneurs who catch its spirit, raise money, recruit their neighbors, find land, select families, and build houses. Along the way these people can get guidance from Habitat for Humanity International staff, but that's no substitute for local initiative. Our Towns Habitat is a somewhat unique example of home-grown Habitat. The current mayor of Davidson, a professor at Davidson College, and others, started Habitat in Davidson in 1988. Ten miles north, Henry Eddy, Ben Thomas, Dave Violette, and others launched Mooresville Lake Norman Habitat in 1991 and soon found themselves building not only in Mooresville, north of Davidson, but also in Huntersville, south of Davidson. Both affiliates were then competing for money and volunteers, which made little sense. By 1993 it dawned on some members of both boards that merging their Habitat affiliates might make more sense. Finally, in 1994, after considerable discussion and some tension, a merger took place and Our Towns Habitat was born.

In my opinion, Habitat's work in the United States today would be strengthened if more affiliates merged, but the organization's leadership has been focused primarily on numbers. Millard's assumption was the more affiliates the better, even though in the past three years up to 25 percent of our affiliates have built no houses. The new and more dynamic affiliate created by the merger of Davidson and Mooresville in 1994 has tripled its annual rate of house building.

I joined Our Towns' board after that merger was accomplished. The affiliate's office was a large closet in the back of a small building on Main Street in Davidson, where it operated a small thrift store. It had just hired Connie Millsaps as its first executive director and arranged to move across Main Street into a large house leased from Davidson College. This facility would support two offices on the second floor and a meeting room and/or workroom. The ground floor would house the thrift store, doubling its space. I remember joining Henry's gang to prepare the space for the store. Ron Bishop, who had just joined Henry's Over-the-Hill Gang, frequently recalls how he was standing near the top of a ten-foot ladder when I approached below and asked him to join our board. Ron reports that as I held his ladder there seemed to be an implied threat should he decline. I recruit Habitat volunteers any way I can.

When I joined the board, recruiting new board members was a central concern. Many of the existing board members were burned out from the merger and the years they had spent on their respective boards. Unless founding board members focus on attracting others, infusing them with excitement, and sharing the decision making, an affiliate is apt to flounder and may die. Many of the Habitat affiliates that are not building houses today find themselves in this same predicament, with dying boards. It was obvious to me and to others on Our Towns' board that our current president had less time to give to the affiliate because of job pressures or Habitat burnout or both. He was often unavailable, and the new executive director had little support. I told the executive director that I would take on the role of board president if no one else wanted it. In the summer of 1995, the board elected me as its president.

I did not know what I was facing. Lots were scarce. Fund-raising had peaked. Our family selection committee struggled to find qualified families, and we could not seem to build more than four or five houses per year on a consistent basis.

Yet Our Towns Habitat had some great assets. Bill Giduz, volunteering with Davidson Habitat from its inception, brought remarkable communication skills and ability and produced *The Humanitarian*, Our Towns' excellent quarterly newsletter. Ben Thomas, a Mooresville attorney, handled all of the affiliate's legal work and closings on a pro bono basis. Dave Violette, from Mooresville, devoted hours to family

selection and volunteered on our electrical crew. Our thrift store, supported by many volunteers from the Pines, Davidson's retirement community, sold gently used items and generated tens of thousands of
dollars a year in support of house building. Davidson College sold
lots to the affiliate at bargain prices, and its students often joined our
Saturday work teams. Officials in all four towns looked favorably
on Habitat's work and guided us on issues of zoning, planning, and
inspections. And last but not least, Henry Eddy and his friends could
build houses.

What we lacked was a strong board and a vision for the future. So in
the spring of 1996, the board spent an afternoon and evening at our
house and went through a formal strategic planning process. We examined the affiliate's strengths and weaknesses, opportunities and threats.
We made lists of possible actions for each committee to consider, and
we focused our mission of creating the partnerships and resources necessary to eliminate poverty housing in the four towns. Our strategy was
to become "the volunteer organization of choice" so that at a minimum
we could increase our house building by at least one house per year.
This strategy required more attention to organizing and thanking our
volunteers, as well as a greater outreach to churches and other community organizations.

Reflecting now on Our Towns' simple and straightforward statement of mission and strategy, I am reminded that our international
board of directors and staff are increasingly coming to the conclusion
that creating partnerships with other housing and microfinance organizations is necessary for Habitat to be effective around the world. The
issues of poverty housing are so large that Habitat's current efforts,
which produce a house somewhere in the world every twenty-four
minutes, or twenty thousand houses per year, fall far short of meeting
the need. But it takes confidence to enter partnerships, as well as skill
and a certain mind-set that Habitat for Humanity International is just
beginning to develop.

I remained president of Our Towns Habitat until I resigned in the
fall of 2001, just after my election as chair of the international board.
From the spring of 1996 until the fall of 2001, I fulfilled different roles
on the international board: treasurer and chair of the Finance Committee, chair of the Strategic Planning Committee, chair of the USA/Canada
Subcommittee, and chair of the U.S. Council. During this time, I was
also working at the grass roots with Our Towns Habitat, presiding over
its board but also finding and acquiring property to subdivide into lots;

serving as a house leader once or twice a year; and meeting with families falling behind on their mortgages.

Habitat for Humanity is unique in that respect. As a volunteer you can work on several different levels in the organization simultaneously. Staying close to Habitat's grass roots, being grounded in the everyday issues faced by affiliates, homeowners, and volunteers, equipped me to be a more effective member of the international board.

After my first international board meeting in Manila in February 1996, I adopted another strategy to increase my effectiveness as a board member and committed to travel at least a week in advance of any board meeting outside the United States and build with Habitat families in those countries.

5

TWICE THE TROUBLE,
TWICE THE FUN

Amy Leonard, our first child, was born in Chicago on April 18, 1964. When Judy entered South Chicago Hospital in labor, Chicago still seemed to be in winter's grasp. A few days later when I brought Amy and Judy home to our university apartment, spring had arrived. So I always associate Amy's birth with the coming of spring; warmer, brighter days; and the greening of trees and the budding of flowers.

Two years and almost two months later, we were expecting our second child. I was in a meeting in my office at Trinity Presbyterian Church when Judy knocked on the door and motioned for me to step into the hall. I tolerate interruptions, but not very well. Going to the door, I noticed Judy had tears in her eyes. Then she told me we were having not one child but two. In a stroke of genius not forgotten, I said, "Good, we will have two tax deductions." With that observation, I turned and went back to my meeting and Judy ran down the hall to the church administrator's office crying.

After a few minutes, the shock of Judy's news and my reaction hit me head-on, and I went to find Judy. Ten days later we were blessed with the arrival of identical twin boys, Jon and Andy, and life has never been the same. A guide for parents of twins popular at that time was titled *Twice the Trouble, Twice the Fun.*

When I think about serving as president of Our Towns Habitat and on the international board at the same time, twice the trouble and twice the fun seems like a fit title for what I have experienced with Habitat. Both the boys and Habitat have brought well over twice the fun into our lives. But when I agreed to serve on the board of Our Towns Habitat, I had no idea that three months later Buck Blankenship would be sitting in my living room asking if he could nominate me as a director on the international board.

Before Buck came into my life, retirement from Centex Real Estate Corporation was my primary focus. One of my goals was to retire at age fifty-five, and part of the reason was that my mother had died at forty-one and my father at sixty, both with heart disease. It was clear from my medical history that I shared those same genes. I did not want to die with my Centex jacket on, and Judy and I wanted time to travel, sail, and spoil our grandchildren. In home building, as in other businesses, loyalty is highly valued, and often those who choose to leave are relieved of their keys and ushered to the door at the moment they declare their intention. That's why retirement took some thought and planning. Before announcing my intention to retire, I wanted to be prepared to do so the next day.

So I was surprised in May 1994, eight months before my fifty-fifth birthday, to learn from Tim Eller, Centex Homes' president, that he wanted two years notice before I retired. Hearing that, I told Tim to consider himself notified, and together we began to assess the Centex team and decide on my successor. This process took several months, and when Tim chose Bob Hillmann, my Raleigh Division president, to assume my role, I could not have been more pleased. Then Bob and I had to go through a similar process to replace him, and on and on until three internal promotions were planned as a result of my retirement. Once these positions were set, each employee involved in the changes began to learn his new responsibilities while training his successor. The fact that Centex's management team could fill each of these positions internally is a powerful testimony to its strength.

Beyond asking for two years notice, Centex had a couple of other surprises in store for me. One was a consulting and non-compete agreement that lasted four years beyond my retirement and provided health benefits as well as modest compensation, all in return for very few demands on my time. The second surprise was my retirement party. Having joined Centex in 1987, I still felt like a relative newcomer to the company and team. Not being based in the Dallas home office and not having shared the company's history with the officers there, I felt more like a distant cousin than a beloved brother.

The party was supposed to be a surprise, but they did have to tell me to reserve a Friday night in September. Here is the amazing part: Centex reserved a country club in Charlotte and then flew the entire corporate team—including chairman and CEO Larry Hirsch and all the division presidents who reported to me or whom I had mentored—and their spouses to this party. Working through Judy, Centex also invited all of our children and their spouses and obtained pictures and life stories for the royal roast they planned.

It was a no-holds-barred event. Jay Kopel, a former Crosland employee who is now a Centex executive vice president, said he was going to make his comments the way I would do it. Then he divided the party into five groups with assignments to report back on my strengths and weaknesses. Bob Hillmann told everyone I never left the ministry—I just changed pulpits. Bill Gillilan, Centex's president, observed that Judy had recruited me away from Centex to join her social services enterprise. Larry Hirsch used slides and reported that I had worked for Cross Land (Crosland), where I had come up with unique townhouse designs (each of the townhouses in the slide show featured a cross mounted at the roof peak), and that I had become concerned when I heard that Sin-Tex (Centex) wanted to buy Cross Land. It went downhill from there.

But I always will have prominently displayed in my living room the leaded glass sculpture I received that night. It is in the shape of a circle with the outline of a house in its center. The inscription reads, "He made for himself a home in our hearts." The feeling is mutual.

It was in large part because of Centex's work with Habitat for Humanity that Buck Blankenship appeared not long after my retirement party. Buck asked about my willingness to serve on Habitat's international board, and I inquired about time and commitment. Buck left an application with questions about my Christian experience, church and community involvement, professional experiences, Habitat experiences, my goals for the future, the assets I might bring to Habitat, and the way Habitat might help me achieve my goals. In other words, this was a fairly serious application. Sometime after returning the application, I received a call from Carl Umland and Carol Freeland, who introduced themselves as directors and members of the Board Service Committee. They reviewed my application, asked questions, and left me with the impression that the Board Service Committee would recommend my name to the full board for election as a new director. That election was held in November, and I was invited to attend my first board meeting in Manila in February 1996.

Judy and I had traveled internationally before Habitat, but it was tourist travel. Sightseeing and history were our prime interests. At different times, we had been to England, Greece, Italy, Holland, Switzerland, and France. We had also been to Hawaii and Alaska and made two trips to Jamaica and the Caribbean Islands. None of these trips prepared us for Manila, its mass of humanity, pollution, tin shacks, motor scooters, jitneys, buses, armed guards in hotels and stores, and all the other sights and smells of this large city.

The only earlier travel experience that offered even a hint of the challenges faced in developing countries was our first trip to Jamaica twenty years earlier. There we saw armed guards at the airport, which was surrounded by fencing topped with barbed wire. We were accosted by islanders aggressively selling their wares outside the resort's walls. One of these sellers called himself Cheap Charlie. Relieved to return to the United States after that visit, I wrote an ode to Cheap Charlie:

> Hey, mon!
> Let's make a deal.
> Come, lady!
> See my baskets.
> I'm Cheap Charlie.
>
> Cheap Charlie is everywhere,
> In the park,
> Along the road,
> By the sea.
> He sells,
> He trades,
> He deals,
> He bargains.
>
> He's five,
> Fifteen,
> Four,
> Or forty.
> Before he can read,
> He can sell.

Before he can write,
He can bargain.

Cheap Charlie is
Neither dumb nor cheap.
Streetwise, world wise,
Up at sunrise,
He survives.

In 1976 I had no clue about the number of countries where barter was the primary source of livelihood, or about the places in the world where begging was one's only hope. Years later, through Habitat for Humanity, I met beggars in India who were more aggressive and more frightening than the sellers in Jamaica. Manila opened my eyes and changed my perspective on life.

I had never seen eighteen- and twenty-year-olds dressed in fatigues, armed with submachine guns, guarding hotel lobbies and the doors of almost every retail establishment. I had never seen such traffic congestion and belches of exhaust from scooters, buses, and taxis, so much exhaust that many pedestrians covered their faces with handkerchiefs or masks. I had never seen children playing beside open sewers or tin shacks with roofs held on by piles of old rubber tires. I had never experienced a family's graciously moving out of their home to provide a place for me to sleep at night. In the midst of poverty and deprivation, I had never seen women leading their families in morning prayers and songs of thanksgiving and praise. I had never discerned the true difference between the riches of the spirit and the riches of this world. Manila changed all that for me.

When you travel with Habitat, you observe and experience society and culture at multiple levels. When we returned from Rotaryville, a Habitat village overlooking one of Manila's bays, Cardinal Sin welcomed our board members to the "House of Sin." Eighty-five percent of the population of the Philippines is Catholic, and the support of the Catholic Church and its cardinal is critical to Habitat's work there. After an open discussion with the cardinal, made possible by Antonio B. (Sonny) de Los Reyes, an international board member and a prominent lay leader in the Catholic Church, the board dined at the home of U.S. Ambassador John Negroponte and his wife, Diana, who later joined our board. Ambassador Negroponte and his wife are staunch supporters of Habitat. At dinner that evening an employee of the United States

Agency for International Development (USAID) told me that the Filipinos were overfishing their coastal waters and that this practice coupled with continued high birth rates spelled trouble for an already suffering economy and people.

After living in the city of Manila for several days and visiting Habitat's work there, our board moved to a retreat center in the country for its meeting. This was the only board meeting during my eight years that Millard missed. Nine other members were absent as well. That left eighteen of us to conduct the business of the board. We approved some new affiliates, bringing the total to 1,219 affiliates in the United States and 390 campus chapters. That year, 1995, Habitat had built 3,300 houses in the United States and 7,000 in other countries. When I left the board in November of 2003, the annual rates of production in the United States and abroad essentially had doubled.

The treasurer noted that Habitat ended 1995 with $150,000 of borrowed funds. That number had jumped to $10.6 million late in 2003 and was reflective of program growth surpassing revenue growth in Habitat's more recent years. In Manila, the board approved a contingency plan that would kick in if changes in revenue or expenses varied over $3 million from the approved budget. We also approved a search committee to find a senior vice president of programs. I was one of two at-large members of the board the chair appointed to this committee.

As a new board member, the most interesting aspect of the Manila meeting was a session on globalization in which members divided into different groups and discussed Habitat case studies from different parts of the world. Our board chair, Wayne Walker, was determined to move Habitat for Humanity from the perspective of a U.S. corporation with a few international board members doing business around the world to that of a truly global company sensitive to cultural differences and committed to diversity that happened to have U.S. headquarters. In five case studies the board examined Habitat's operations around the world.

We learned about the dangers of a strong charismatic leader and the possible corruption of a fledgling national organization. We discussed the impact of starting in a new country without the necessary research and the consequences of not understanding and possibly disrespecting the local culture. We examined a weak U.S. affiliate with burned-out board members willing to accept government funds at any cost. We focused on a national organization in Africa still dominated by U.S. nationals employed by Habitat International, experiencing mistrust and poor relations with local affiliates. Finally, we studied the dilemma of a

Christian organization in a non-Christian country and the consequences of publicly giving Bibles to families in a region where people are ostracized and sometimes attacked for affiliation with Christianity. Underlying each of these cases were real Habitat experiences. Names had been changed to protect the guilty.

This discussion sensitized us to the complexity of Habitat's work around the world. The need to strengthen our work at local and national levels and align our local, national, and international objectives and resources seemed paramount. Goodwill and good intentions would be no substitute for thoughtful, competent management in the years ahead. Habitat for Humanity needed both, and most of all we needed to remove our U.S. glasses and look at the world through wider lenses.

A photographed prayer captured the wisdom and understanding that are so difficult to grasp in the United States and other Western countries:

He asked for strength that he might achieve; he was made weak that he might obey.

He asked for health that he might do greater things; he was given infirmity that he might do better things.

He asked for riches that he might be happy; he was given poverty that he might be wise.

He asked for power that he might have the praise of men; he was given weakness that he might feel the need of God.

He asked for all things that he might enjoy life; he was given life that he might enjoy all things.

He has received nothing that he asked for, all that he hoped for. His prayer is answered. He is most blessed.

In this prayer is the paradox of a world searching for power and riches but needing mostly love and grace. My prayer for Habitat for Humanity is to always be an instrument of love and grace.

6

A FAMILY HOUSE

Judy is excellent at crazy ideas. She thought the trips to the Jimmy Carter Work Projects and a blitz build with the Lynchburg, Virginia, affiliate in September 1995 were so much fun that the Leonard family should sponsor and build a Habitat house. Thanks to 120 acres we had purchased from her grandfather's estate in 1981 and recently sold, funding a Habitat house was not an issue. The question was when and where. Since Judy served on the board of Charlotte Habitat and it was her idea, Charlotte was the logical place. And the earliest possible time was a month after we returned from the Habitat International board meeting in Manila.

But this was not just a commitment of financial resources; it was also a commitment to recruit the volunteers and build the house in a week. When we returned from Manila, Charlotte Habitat had the foundation ready for the Leonard House at 1005 Allen Street, and we had to get to work.

I finished high school with a negative view of my family. My mom died without warning four days before Christmas and a month before my twelfth birthday. It was not until I was thirty years old and Judy and I were in family counseling that I got a handle on the impact my mother's death had on me. I knew the impact my stepmother had, and it was not good. But, basically as a defensive mechanism, I had blocked out most of my childhood memories and had unconsciously adopted the view that women cannot be trusted because they will leave you. On the other hand, Dad appeared to me as a loser, someone who smoked and drank too much, a guy with good ideas that others often swiped. From my dad I absorbed a fear of failure, a strong motivating force in my life.

Because my dad and stepmother moved to another town, I did not live at home during my senior year in high school. Because of an untenable relationship with my stepmother, I never spent another night in their home even during college. So I entered fatherhood with some very definite ideas about family. Mainly, I would get my children through college as long as they also worked and contributed. After that, they would be on their own. As much as I loved and cared for them while they were growing up, I fully expected them to move out, marry, go their way, and leave us alone.

Judy taught me a lot about family, about love that is both tender and tough, about hanging in and sweating the details in the children's lives and our own lives every day. I have learned a lot about family from my children, who, while they have finished college, bought their own homes, and started their own families, have never left us out of the circle of love and bonds of trust and respect. When I call on them to help build a Habitat house or for any other reason, they come.

So a month after returning from Manila, the Leonard family and friends built a house with Thoat Pham and Hong Ngyuen and their six daughters—and their adult son, who helped with the building but would not live in the house. But in some ways, we were also building the house for us, to celebrate our family and friends, share the good news of Habitat, and just enjoy a good old blitz build. Jon and Elizabeth came. Andy and Kelly came. Judy's sister, Helen, and her husband, Jimmy, and daughter, Dana, drove from Georgia and spent the week with us. Our brother-in-law Larry McGee flew in from Pittsburgh. My third cousin, Ed Leonard, drove from Massachusetts. The Over-the-Hill Gang came from Mooresville. Bob Lowke, a friend from the Church in the City days, brought his wife, Jeanne, and drove from Orlando, Florida. I can't count the number of Charlotte friends, such as Marvin and Pattie Bethune, Hal and Cynthia Curry, and Steve and Glenda Helms, who took most of their week to work together on this house.

Cynthia Curry organized snacks and lunch for the six days we worked. Pattie Bethune and her children, John and Laura, cooked an evening meal for our out-of-town guests and babysat. The logistics of a blitz build are as daunting and taxing as the build itself.

I needed a good construction manager who loved people to get us through that week. Roger Johnston started working as a warranty service man for the John Crosland Company in the 1980s. Roger always excelled at customer service because he cared for people, and he excelled at this work because by experience he had learned every aspect of building, including the plumbing and electrical trades. At the time I asked Roger to volunteer on the Leonard house, he was a construction manager for Centex, overseeing the work in several subdivisions. But he gladly joined us, and because of his leadership, before nightfall on the first day, we built and raised the exterior and interior walls, installed the windows and doors, erected the trusses, and sheathed and dried in the roof. No one got mad or felt hurt or left out—a tribute to Roger's ability to teach and to work with people. Since that day, Roger has worked with me on many more houses, and always his talent for leading volunteers amazes me.

It's interesting that in Charlotte, the Queen City of the New South, we were building a Habitat house for a family from Vietnam. But after the Vietnam War, Charlotte became a port city for families escaping the communist regime, and Thoat and Hong were part of that refugee stream. In fact, by 1995 almost a fourth of the families working with Charlotte Habitat came from Southeast Asia. We sometimes forget, but there is an international aspect of Habitat just in the United States. Immigrants from Somalia, Vietnam, Cambodia, Central America, and Bosnia, to mention a few, have all been partners in Habitat's work and the recipients of homes that to them are castles they had believed possible only in their dreams.

A couple has never smiled or looked more lovingly into each other's face than Thoat and Hong, nor worked harder on their home. The prayers, tears, and joy we shared during the dedication of their home under the oak tree in their backyard washed away the blisters and bruises of the build. That day both the Leonard family and friends and the Pham and Ngyuen family were touched and transformed by God's grace. Perhaps then you can share the shock Judy and I felt when, several months later, Thoat left Hong for another woman and Hong's ability to repay the mortgage became an immediate concern. Hong ultimately sold that house on Allen Street, but only after she and her daughters made the payments for several years and through hard work achieved even greater economic success.

Not all Habitat stories have good endings. Through their hard work, Hong and her children averted disaster. But a Habitat family in Davidson lost their home when they refinanced the Habitat 0 percent loan with a predatory lender who promised additional money to pay for funereal expenses and other credit card debt along with an 11 percent new mortgage loan. Fortunately, these examples are the exceptions, and Habitat affiliates are working to keep them that way through more emphasis on homeowner consumer education prior to the house dedications and title transfers.

One of the most effective homeowner educational programs is one called Fiscal Therapy, developed and run by Knoxville Habitat for Humanity. Fiscal Therapy is a series of classes focused on family budgets, credit card debt, mortgage loans, insurance, wills, and home maintenance. These classes are part of the requirement for homeowners in the construction phase of their homes. Credit toward their sweat equity is given for attending the Fiscal Therapy classes. Many U.S. affiliates have adopted similar programs and have found that this up-front investment in homeowner education pays dividends through timelier mortgage repayments and better home maintenance.

I attended a homeowner class Judy developed for Our Towns Habitat and I was surprised when one of the prospective homeowners told the class about negotiating a 50 percent reduction in a loan balance by offering immediate cash payment in lieu of $10 monthly payments over the next several years. This homeowner acted on ideas previously discussed in class, and her report inspired our other homeowners to take control of their finances as well. Amazingly, these homeowners openly shared their financial challenges. The fact that they were building each other's houses at the same time strengthened their bonds and laid the groundwork for a strong community.

We often claim that Habitat for Humanity builds more than houses. As Habitat families work and attend classes together they are also building community and trust that will strengthen and sustain their neighborhoods.

7

THE BEST-LAID PLANS

When an organization is small and just beginning, you can run it out of your back room, which is exactly where in 1976 Habitat for Humanity started—in the back room of Millard Fuller's law office. Today Habitat for Humanity owns two multistory office buildings, a warehouse, the Global Village and Discovery Center, and thirty houses used for volunteers and various offices in Americus, Georgia. But figuratively in many respects, before 2005 we were still operating out of Millard Fuller's back room.

Millard was our leader. He supplied the vision, charisma, drive, energy, and commitment that propeled Habitat for Humanity forward. Millard saw Habitat as a movement with the mission to actualize the kingdom of God daily by working to ensure that everyone on the planet has a simple, decent place to sleep at night. This is a rather large vision to run out of a back room or the economy section of an airplane, where Millard spent 70 percent of his time.

It was instructive for me as a relatively new board member in 1997 to hear the report from John Durrett of McKinsey and Company. John and his colleagues had performed a pro bono study called Project Impact, which examined Habitat's work and organization in depth and recommended changes for the future. John was very direct. He noted that the corporation had no strategy, no integrated set of plans or actions to achieve its mission. The best he could say about our management processes was that they were terrible—no measurements, no timetables, no accountability, no recruiting, no training, and no staff evaluations. He noted that our information and financial systems did not support our decision making.

John continued. He said that the board and staff were divided and that the board and Millard were in conflict. Some board members had told him that Millard was not an effective manager, that he generated more ideas than Habitat could handle, resented being held accountable, and valued loyalty over competence. On the other side, Millard saw the board meddling in staff affairs in unproductive ways and wanting to take over the corporation.

Anyone familiar with nonprofit organizations or churches probably won't discern much new here. In the South, people say the two things you do not want to see being made are sausage and politics. I quickly add Habitat and my church to this list. Close up, the internal struggles and operations bred anything but confidence, and you wonder how in the world this organization manages to keep growing and succeeding, a miracle unfolding right before your eyes.

John gave three recommendations, all of which indicated that Habitat could not continue to be run successfully out of a back room. The staff needed to bring to the board a three- to five-year strategic plan. The staff had to develop an action plan to complement the strategic directions and hold people accountable. Habitat required clearly defined human resource policies and procedures. After John's presentation, a strategic plan was in Habitat's future.

When the board met in Guatemala, Nana Prah, chair of a newly formed strategic planning committee, gave her first report. She led the board through a process to identify the strengths, weaknesses, opportunities, and threats facing the organization. We listed these strengths:

Diversity of the board
Christian focus
Clear vision and mission
Decentralization
Global presence
Trust
Momentum

When the board came to weaknesses, it sounded as if John Durrett's remarks had hit home:

Lack of accountability
Poor quality
Weak management
Unclear values
Too focused on the United States in both program and fund-raising
Too dependent on direct mail, Millard Fuller, and Jimmy Carter
Not collaborative with other organizations
Ineffective in urban areas
Weak in its support of existing affiliates

After a lengthy discussion about not only Habitat's strengths and weaknesses but also its opportunities and threats, the board chose three strategies for the future: building global organizational competency; building, diversifying, and sustaining fund-raising; and increasing house-building numbers. In rereading the minutes from this 1997 Guatemala meeting and its focus on a plan for the future, I was struck by the similarity with many other board discussions since then.

A second strategic plan was developed for 2000–2005 that called for building the next one hundred thousand homes worldwide, expanding Habitat operations to one hundred countries, and raising an extra $500 million to accomplish the house-building and expansion goals. This plan also identified and defined four strategic objectives critical for achieving the above goals: leadership, innovation, advocacy, and capacity building. At my final board meeting in New Zealand in November 2003, guess what: another strategic plan was being formulated, again focusing on strengthening our global presence, fund-raising, and management.

Millard told me in New Zealand that he saw no value in the 2000–2005 strategic plan and had little use for the new one under discussion, except for his thought that we needed to build another two hundred thousand houses by 2011, Habitat's thirty-fifth anniversary. Millard saw value in loyalty and in people following his lead and carrying out their assigned tasks. He liked the back room approach, and he either left the room or fell asleep when the board begun to discuss the strategic plan. A new board member told me, with a look of astonishment on her face, that she had never attended a board meeting in which the CEO of the corporation wasn't present or didn't participate. Welcome to Habitat's back-room office, where the real plans were made and where the best-laid plans often were ignored.

8

LESSONS AND ELECTIONS

When the Habitat for Humanity international board gathered in Cleveland, Ohio, in October 1997, my second year as a director and my one-year term as treasurer were ending. The time had passed quickly. As treasurer, I had been able to work with Millard Fuller, his staff, and the Finance Committee to craft a reserve policy for the corporation. Millard steadfastly had rejected such policies in the past, arguing that the house mortgages held by the affiliates provided all the reserves and endowments Habitat required. Why leave funds in an investment account when Habitat could build more houses, when the need for simple, decent houses was so great?

That was a difficult argument to rebut. The fact that the mortgages were owned by the affiliates and not Habitat for Humanity International, however, was not lost on board members. The fact that affiliates such as Homestead, Florida, and Uptown Chicago had problems large enough to discredit their parent organization, Habitat for Humanity International, was not lost on Millard, especially since he had to report on unbudgeted loans and grants to these affiliates of over $500,000. So the Finance Committee and staff drafted a reserve policy that included funds for affiliate emergencies as well as an opportunity fund for starting new ventures. This was a modest reserve equal to three months' operating budget and was to be funded over three years. I helped the board see the importance of the loans to Homestead and Uptown Chicago, and Millard gave up his objection to a reserve fund. The board learned later that both the opportunity fund and the emergency fund needed governing parameters and guidelines as well. Otherwise, these funds simply became additional sources for uncontrolled and unplanned spending by the president and his staff.

Most organizations have nominating committees that recommend new directors as well as officers. Habitat for Humanity International has a Board Service Committee whose members are elected by the board, which then selects its own chair. All other committee chairs and members are appointed to their positions by the chair of the board with board approval. The Board Service Committee has the most significant responsibility among our board committees, for it not only nominates new directors and officers but also consults with existing directors on their performance. The task is made more difficult by the board's commitment to diversity, not only in terms of gender and race but also in terms of strong international representation. This committee's work goes on year-round and culminates at the fall board meeting with the election of directors and officers.

Prior to the meeting in Cleveland, I had been asked by the Board Service Committee to serve another term as treasurer. The board had amended its bylaws the previous year to increase an officer's term from one to two years.

It had been my experience from the October 1996 election that once the Board Service Committee recommended the officers' slate, the board rubber-stamped it and the new officers were set. I was surprised, therefore, that after receiving the board service report in Cleveland, board members discussed voting on the officer recommendations one by one. Then the chair of the Board Service Committee, Dick Celeste, a former governor of Ohio and soon to become the U.S. ambassador to India, asked the current board chair, Wayne Walker, to leave the room, which he did. It quickly became apparent that the board was divided between those who wanted Wayne to be reelected to a two-year term and those totally opposed to his reelection. It had been clear since the Americus meeting in the spring of 1997 and the McKinsey report by John Durrett that there was significant tension between Millard and the board. Now apparently some members believed Wayne Walker was a primary source of that tension. The discussion continued for more than an hour, and toward the end Lyle Hanna, a board member, walked behind my chair and in a whisper asked me if he could nominate me for board chair. My approach to Habitat had been to do as asked. I told Lyle he could nominate me, and he did. Then I left the room.

I ran into Wayne Walker in the men's bathroom, and I told him why I had been sent out of the room. He didn't take the news happily. We waited in the hall, and fifteen minutes passed before Patsy Bonsal joined us. She too had been nominated for chair. We now had three "chairs to be" standing in the hall with no idea what was going on inside the boardroom.

Another hour passed before Wayne, Patsy, and I were re-called. In our absence, the board had agreed to amend the bylaws, reversing the prior year's actions and limiting a term of office to one year. If this amendment passed, the board would elect the slate proposed by the Board Service Committee. A potential problem was that a two-thirds affirmative vote was required to change the bylaws, and the votes of the "chairs to be" were needed for that change. Otherwise, the board was at an impasse. Patsy and I voted with the board, and Wayne abstained. It was an unhappy ending to an unhappy process.

My relationship with Wayne was now strained. The board, disgruntled about being put in what it considered an untenable position, directed the Board Service Committee for all future officer elections to recommend at least two people for each position. Obviously the board members remaining in the room did not share the pain of those of us sitting outside its doors while our qualifications for an office were debated. The request for future competitive elections ensured that the pain would be repeated annually, bringing disharmony to a board in need of harmony.

Maybe it's worth noting that this was not the first election I had lost. In 1969 I ran for city council in Charlotte. My campaign theme was "Charlotte Hurts: Paul Leonard Can Help." All my campaign signs featured "Charlotte Hurts" in large, bold, easily readable letters, while my name, Paul Leonard, was in a smaller font and lost in the ad. After a hard-fought race for one of seven at-large council seats, I came in tenth in a field of fourteen. In a post-election analysis, I told several people that I would have won the election hands down if I had been on the ballot as Charlotte Hurts.

Five years later, on March 24, 1974, I received a letter from Nashville, Tennessee, signed by Charles M. Hurts, telling me he had heard I used his wife's name in my campaign and threatening legal action. Enclosed with the letter was a newspaper clipping advertising Charlotte Hurts in concert at a piano bar in Nashville. I didn't know whether to laugh or call an attorney. Three weeks later a second letter arrived from Arlington, Virginia. This letter was from Charlotte herself. She explained that she wasn't going to sue me and reported that she was returning to Pine Bluff, Arkansas, to run for city council. I was just starting to discover which joker had sent these letters when I received another card from Richmond, Virginia, thanking me for the change I had brought in her life. She had lost the election in Pine Bluff and said it was probably to be expected when you have a Hurt in your campaign. She wanted me to know she had moved on to other things, earned a law degree through a correspondence course, and joined the law firm of Myass, Hurts, and How.

What I learned from the Charlotte election experience is that friends (two of them had sent the three letters), campaign themes, and posters need to be chosen carefully. What I learned from the Habitat election is that I had one more year as treasurer and, based on the bylaws, would not be eligible for election to another office in the fall of 1998. So that fall we had a competitive election, and somewhat surprisingly, Mick Kicklighter, a retired three-star general who had joined the board only eighteen months before, was elected as board chair for a one-year term.

Mick began to heal the rift between Millard and the board, and he worked overtime to bring peace to our meetings and deliberations. Harsh words were no longer spoken, and most of the difficult decisions were forged among the officers and Millard outside the range of our board meetings.

Mick appointed me chair of the Strategic Planning Committee to focus on an overlooked and neglected aspect of the board's work. I inherited a staff-written plan that grew out of our 1997 discussions in Guatemala and featured three objectives: invest in human resources, develop a more businesslike culture, and increase Habitat for Humanity's global impact. The words sounded right, but the plan was not integrated into the organization's budget or operations. There were no measures, benchmarks, or quantifiable goals. Fortunately for me and for the board, Mick had engaged the services of a board consultant, Dr. David Nygren, to help the board look carefully at itself and set a future course of action. Dr. Nygren consulted with the Strategic Planning Committee on ways to develop a strategic plan with organization-wide input and ownership.

I should have learned my lesson the first time. In the fall of 1999, I received a call from the Board Service Committee (which was now required to recommend two candidates for each office): Would I stand for election for board chair? Since the board's mandate in 1997, the Board Service Committee had adopted the approach of polling board members a few months before each election to ask for their choices for officers. The two people mentioned the most for each office became the candidates recommended by the committee.

In our intervening spring board meeting, the bylaws governing terms of office had been changed again so that now a term of office would be two years. Mick had done a respectable job in his first year as chair, but his work for the Veteran's Department was quite demanding, and he often wasn't able to give Habitat for Humanity the attention it needed. I agreed to be nominated, and on election day, Mick and I found ourselves in the hall for an hour or more while the board voted and voted and voted. Finally, we were called back into the boardroom, and his reelection as chair was announced.

Mick was gracious in his victory. I was hurt, and Judy was mad. But we got over it, and Mick reappointed me as chair of the Strategic Planning Committee and added a second task of chairing the USA/Canada Subcommittee.

Apparently three is a magic number. In the fall of 2001, Jim Copeland, who chaired the Board Service Committee, called and asked me to run for board chair. I told Jim I had to think hard before putting myself through that process again. A few days later, I decided to run under the condition that the other nominee, vice chair Mark Korell, and I would not have to leave the room while the vote was taken. Jim agreed to this condition, and then to my delight the board elected me to a two-year term as chair.

In hindsight, it was worth the wait. Mick brought unity to the board so that when I took office, the board was ready to move forward on many issues that had been discussed but not acted on for several years. Having served on so many committees and task forces and worked with most board members, I was better prepared to lead and knew what I needed to accomplish. I began immediately to select my committee chairs, appoint committees, and spell out a plan and expectations for the next two years.

9

A VOLUNTEER
HOME-BUILDING COMPANY

One day in 1994 Judy and I were explaining Habitat to Victor, a Russian visitor in our home. Victor was in the United States as a participant in a USAID program. He could not understand why we worked with Habitat for no pay. The idea of volunteering to build a house for strangers was a totally foreign concept to him. Later, during our own travels in India, we found no volunteers at work on Habitat building sites. And we have been told by Guatemalans that it is customary to volunteer assistance to one's extended family, but not to neighbors or other families.

One attribute of Americans that we need most to celebrate is our willingness to help others, to volunteer countless hours and donate freely to the work of nonprofit organizations. It takes between eighteen hundred and two thousand volunteer hours to complete a Habitat house in the United States. Those hours may be supplied by a dedicated group of thirty individuals working five or six ten-hour days to build a house in a week. Or they may be supplied by two hundred or more people who show up on fourteen to sixteen Saturdays to build. However it happens, Habitat and its company of volunteers build six thousand houses a year in the United States and in the process contribute over nine million hours of free labor.

For more than ten years, Bill Hladik, who is retired, has been a construction volunteer for Our Towns Habitat. Bill has served on the board of directors during part of that time, but his real love is construction. On his own, Bill learned to wire a house. He then designed a simplified system for teaching other volunteers his skills. Bill provides diagrams detailing each electrical circuit, including the location of lights, receptacles, and switches. A two-person volunteer team recruited and trained by Bill then wires a circuit. Bill will have three to four teams working in each house. Bill's crews have wired over sixty houses with the supervision of a licensed electrician who permits and inspects each house.

But Bill doesn't stop with the electrical wiring. He has also put all of the affiliate's house plans on computer, and he uses this program to estimate the framing lumber required for each house. With his computer designs, Bill details the assembly of wall, window, and door components, eliminating the guesswork for other volunteers who might be unfamiliar with house framing. In his spare time, Bill has also been known to pick up the lumber and pre-build the window and door components for a number of houses.

One might think that Bill Hladik's volunteer commitment and hours of service to Habitat are unusual. But people like Bill Hladik volunteer in almost every affiliate and at Habitat headquarters in Americus, where at any given time volunteers will be living and working as part of our international staff. To professional builders this ragtag volunteer building company must at first glance seem laughable. It did to me before I joined Habitat.

Yet the spirit of Habitat's volunteers is anything but laughable. For my sixtieth birthday at a surprise party Judy arranged, my friends donated almost enough funds to build a Habitat house. When the time came to build the house, Judy insisted I lead the build and invite our friends to work with us. On the scheduled start date, December 13, 2003, there was a heavy downpour, and the temperature hovered around 38 degrees.

My vote was to cancel the day's activities, but at 6:00 a.m., when I called the local construction leader and a few of the regular volunteers, they wanted to work. I have never been so cold or wet. Twenty people showed up, and by noon we had framed all the walls. Two inches of water lay on the wooden subfloor. I asked Bob Gates, a friend and masonry contractor who was working beside me, if his laborers would show up for work on a day such as this.

"Haven't you heard of the three-drop rule?" Bob asked.

I said I hadn't.

"My masons get up in the morning and hold out a trowel," Bob said. "If three drops of rain fall on it in thirty minutes, they don't work!"

Two inches of rain did not dampen the spirit and work of those volunteers.

Thinking about that day, I am reminded of another day on a Habitat site when the sun was shining and the heat shimmering. The drywall finishers hired by Habitat were sanding the walls, and dust flew in every direction. While the finishers worked inside, Habitat volunteers installed siding and trim outside. About the middle of the afternoon, one of the finishers emerged from the house. He was African-American, and the layer of white drywall dust coating him gave him a ghostlike appearance. As he wiped his brow, I could sense his tiredness, but he kept looking back at the house as if he were puzzled. Then he asked me, "Why are all these people smiling?"

One does not have to spend much time on a typical construction site to understand that frowns and oaths rule there. But not at this house. Smiles everywhere, enough smiles to convince this experienced drywall finisher that something different was happening. It was a good question: Why were all those people smiling? And why do they keep showing up in the heat, cold, rain, and wind to volunteer their time? I know. It changes their own lives and as long as they keep coming, there is still hope for the soul and spirit of America and for the families in need of a simple, decent place to live.

10

LOCATION, LOCATION, LOCATION

"Location, location, location" is the mantra of the real estate industry. It is somewhat akin to an oft-repeated political reminder, "It's the economy, stupid!" In real estate, a good location supersedes almost any other attribute and through the years overcomes down markets and even poor management. During my twenty-two years in home building and development, I learned about location through both good and bad decisions and used that knowledge to acquire an ideal location for my present home. Judy and I now live in Davidson, North Carolina, a small college town, home to my alma mater where we can walk less than four blocks on any winter evening and see my Davidson Wildcats basketball team take on the Citadel Bulldogs or VMI Cadets at Baker Sports Complex. Or I can sit on my deck and hear the cheers and announcer from a Saturday afternoon football game.

Davidson is my dream location because had it not been for Davidson College, my life story would have had a completely different twist. Growing up in a family not privileged to experience college, it is easy to appreciate the value of a college education. Davidson College, its professors, its history, and my experiences there reside close to my heart. Davidson is about as close to heaven as I hope to get. There is only one problem. Habitat for Humanity has trumped Davidson in its impact on my life. Now when I'm home sitting on that nice deck and gazing at the canopy of trees and the Carolina blue sky, I think about Billy in Belfast, Gladys in Baanuase, A. K. in Durban, Chantal in Haiti, Sangeetha in Bangalore, Sonny in Manila, Juan in Xela, and so many others living in locations and circumstances much less favorable than mine. So my perception of location has been altered radically, as has my view of the world, and now every chance I get I try to change the perception of others as well.

In the spring of 2003, I was invited to give the commencement address to the graduating class of Queens University of Charlotte. In J. K. Footlick's book *Awakening*, Queens University chairman Hugh McColl is quoted as telling students at the University of Kansas, in a 1998 speech, "We all belong to three groups—our work, our family, and the rest of the people who live in the place where we live." Using McColl's statement to set up my challenge to the Queens graduates, here is part of that morning's speech.

> It is my observation that today the most difficult challenge before you and the rest of us is properly to define and understand "the place where we live." We build walls around houses and neighborhoods, we mark city and county limits, and we guard country borders to create places of comfort and security for our families and ourselves. Since 9/11 our country has had to raise its walls, build up its security, and strengthen its armed forces. Yet we must wonder, will this walled and armed path really lead to a more secure and humane future?
>
> There are protective neighborhood walls in Belfast, Northern Ireland, 90 feet high. They are called "peace walls." Some are adorned with the militaristic symbols and standards of the Irish Republican Army, others with those of the Protestant Militia. Belfast has peace walls but no peace. Fareed Zakaria reported in the March 24, 2003, issue of *Newsweek* that in the next fiscal year the United States would spend $322 billion on defense, which turns out to be more than the defense budgets of all other countries in the world combined. Will this lead to peace for us and the world? And can America have peace if the world's other countries do not?
>
> . . . In October 2001, an article in the *Charlotte Observer* explored the living conditions in the neighborhoods of Afghanistan and Pakistan that provide the recruiting grounds for terrorists. One short sentence captured the article's message and burned itself into my heart and head. It read, "The children are taught to beg in seven languages." In other

words, the young people growing up in the neighborhoods of these countries have no hope and no future apart from begging.

There are Afghanistans and Pakistans on six continents. As you define the borders for the place you will live, you might prayerfully contemplate the meaning of the grace, the luck, or the circumstance of your own birth and the wonder of the opportunities before you now.

Joe Lowke, a friend from Texas, volunteered for service in Vietnam in the 1960s under threat of the draft. Joe served as an infantry platoon leader and spent nine months under fire in the field. Thinking about our young men and women now in Iraq, I asked Joe recently what influence Vietnam had on the rest of his life. Slowly and thoughtfully, Joe said, "It made me more certain of the grace of God and the preciousness of all life."

Joe added that each day before he led his platoon on a mission, he prayed for God to protect him and his men and to help them not to find anyone to fight or kill. Then after a firefight one night when Joe and his platoon killed and captured some two hundred Viet Cong, they got caught up in the excitement of war. The platoon could not wait for the next day's search-and-destroy mission. It was that day that Joe forgot his prayer. It was also the day Joe was wounded, and later, upon reflection, gleaned this lifelong lesson about the grace of God and the preciousness of all life. Joe used this lesson to define and understand the place where he has lived for the past thirty-five years. May it also be a lesson for you to consider.

In Mr. McColl's 1998 Kansas speech, he said that the success of each group (work, family, and the rest of the people in the place where you live) is dependent on the success of the other two.

"You cannot starve one to the benefit of the other two," he said. "If you try, they will all die."

Where is the place you will live, and how will you define its borders?

In April 2003 in Washington State, Comcast Cable ran two commercials featuring Lance Armstrong racing his bike up a hill, passing his competitors one by one. The voice-over in the first commercial said, "It is not enough to tell people you are committed, to talk about your dedication, strength, grit, or perseverance. You have to prove it." Second commercial, another race, and this voice-over: "No one remembers your name, honors you, or instantly gives you respect just because you show up. You have to earn it."

Your Queens University diploma is your passport as a citizen of the world. . . . May God bless you and Queens University, and may

God bless all the children and families in every country in our world through you!

The *Charlotte Observer* reporter noted the next day that I had delivered a rather somber speech and implied that the graduates were pleased when it was over and they could get their hands on their diplomas. One student later said that she had been both moved by my words and somewhat frightened about the choices and responsibilities she faced.

In the summer of 2003, Fidelity National Asset Management Services (FNAMS) invited me to speak at their national convention in Keystone, Colorado. FNAMS specializes in properties owned or repossessed by lenders and provides a wide range of services, including appraisals, repairs, and sales. All of FNAMS associates would understand "location, location, location," and this mantra provided an opening for the message my Habitat travels had branded on my brain and heart. At Keystone, after thanking the conference attendees for their contributions to Habitat and their house-building efforts, I turned to a theme this audience would understand, the importance of a home to a family.

> You do not have to work very long in a brokerage business before you know implicitly the importance of a house to a family. Most of you see a house's impact through both its foreclosure and ultimate resale. A house is more than shelter, a roof over our heads. It is pride of ownership, the opportunity to live in one place for an extended time and for your children to attend the same schools year after year. It is a chance to build wealth. It is a place of rest and renewal from our day's labor and a safe harbor for moms, dads, and children.

It was easy to move the group's focus from the importance of a home to the importance of location, which they also understood. A cartoon from the *Charlotte Observer* that pictured a dog sitting in an easy chair with the caption "Location, Location, Location" helped make my point.

> That's the most important of the mantras of our business, isn't it? Everyone knows it! And here is an old lazy dog that has found the best location of all, an easy chair. Isn't this exactly what we are looking for, an easy chair, and if possible, on Easy Street?
>
> This conference, called Reaching New Heights, with its noted speakers and leaders is focused on getting us that easy chair: improving

our ability to generate leads, to recruit top agents, to locate and find foreclosures, to finance and close deals, and to profitably operate our businesses.

As I learned during my twenty-two years in the real estate development business, and as you know, nothing beats the right location for any deal. We don't always make the right choices about location, but through market research, demographic analysis, shopping competition, comparing prices, we can come pretty close to determining a good location for any real estate investment. . . .

Speaking of location, the United States of America is not a bad place to live either, given the forethought of our founding fathers and the sacrifices of all who have died and continue to this moment to die to protect our freedom. But here's a fact easily overlooked: No one here chose his or her birthplace. Blessing or curse, it was just laid at our feet. The United States or Liberia, France or Algeria, Canada or Mexico, England or China—wherever the stork landed, you began your life.

We know what a difference location makes in real estate. Think with me about the difference location makes in life estate.

Then I described conditions in Belfast and Ghana and some of the other places visited where location had made a great difference in life estate and concluded with these words:

Since leaving Ghana, two thoughts have stayed with me. The first is Ghana had not yet entered the twentieth century that we in the Western world were leaving. And the second is, except for the grace of God or accident of birthplace, I could be living there with my four children and their families.

When it comes to life estate, location, and birthplace, Gladys Antwi has drawn a short straw or started life at the end of a very long line. There are over two billion people in our world like Gladys who, in respect to life estate, birthplace, and opportunity, have drawn a short straw. Unlike Gladys, who has worked with Habitat for Humanity, no one is working with them to provide any shelter, and their opportunity is to exist on $1 per day. "Reaching new heights" for them would mean earning $2 per day. . . .

At Habitat for Humanity, we are working to awaken people's consciences so that the day will come when it is unacceptable for a child not to have a decent place to sleep at night, no matter where he or she lives or was born, no matter their life estate. But here is our problem.

In 2001 Habitat asked Peter Hart and Associates to conduct a survey. Five hundred Habitat donors, 250 potential donors and 200 corporate giving officers were asked this question: "To whom would you give an extra $100?" The answers were almost identical. Eighty-two to 85 percent would give an extra $100 to a local charity. This suggests that the only location most of us think about or care about is next door or inside our country's border—location, location, location. How likely do you think it is to have peace in a world where two billion people live without safe and decent shelter, water, sanitation, or jobs? Do you think we can support an army big enough to keep peace in such a world?

By 2050 the world's population is expected to stabilize at nine billion. Eight billion of these people will live in Asia, where that population will equal three times the population of North America, Latin America, and Europe combined. What kind of world is this apt to be? . . . Building houses with others around the world, in locations where life estates are not as blessed as ours, is a real way to build peace. . . . Do yourself and our world a favor. The next time you hear, "Location, location, location," remember the gift of your own birthplace, and alter the mantra to "Location, location, compassion."

My message to Queens University students and the FNAMS associates was the same. The preservation of world peace requires that we act on our responsibility as world citizens, sharing the riches and resources we command.

PART 2
PEOPLE AND PLACES

11

MRS. ROBERTSON

I love the lyrics and the beat of Simon and Garfunkel's "Mrs. Robinson." I may not understand the song's meaning (if there is one), but I recalled the song's lyrics when I and other volunteers were building a house with Patricia Robertson:

> And here's to you, Mrs. Robinson,
> Jesus loves you more than you will know.

Her name was Robertson, not Robinson, Mrs. Patricia Robertson—and she lived in Cornelius, North Carolina. I worked with Patricia and her children, Lucretia and Antoine, in the spring of 1997 and was one of more than one hundred volunteers who helped Patricia build her Habitat home in Cornelius. Working on Patricia's house and those of other Habitat families is what lifts my spirit and keeps me engaged with Habitat. Somehow the words of that Simon and Garfunkel song came to me as we were building her house. "Jesus loves you more than you will know. . . . God bless you please, Mrs. Robertson."

A Habitat volunteer asked Mrs. Robertson about her house, and she said, "You don't know how much I want this house. I have never had anything to call my own. It is my dream come true." She also said that the people from Carolina Tractor who sponsored her house had been wonderful. "They've been out here in the rain and in the cold. They were here at the beginning, and I know they'll be here in the end."

A volunteer said, "Patricia's done everything we asked. She and Antoine did all the insulation; we never touched that. Then one time she took a day off from her work to clean up the inside before we painted. It was spotless" (The *Humanitarian*, Spring 1997).

After Patricia moved in, she lovingly cared for her house and yard as well as her neighbors. I was in Patricia's neighborhood on an October day in 1997. This time Judy had invited me to give construction advice on an all-women's house being built next door to Patricia's. The advice I had planned to give was from a sitting position on a stack of lumber in the front yard. The advice I gave was not advice at all. It was hard labor and involved walking on the top wall plates to position roof trusses hoisted by a crane. The trusses were almost in place when a ladder fell with a thud, followed by the sound of running and a muffled cry. I jumped to the floor, rushed outside, and at the rear of the house found Judy lying on her back next to a stack of plywood that her head had barely missed. Her right foot was turned at a strange angle, and her ankle was already swelling. One woman had called 911. I bent to remove Judy's shoe, and she cried, "Don't touch it!"

Then Lucretia, Mrs. Robertson's daughter, shouted, "Mommy, that lady has fallen!" In less than a minute, Patricia came with a blanket and pillow for Judy, who had broken her ankle in the fall. Patricia waited beside us until the medics carried Judy to the ambulance. For months afterward, Patricia always asked about Judy.

"Heaven holds a place for those who pray," or so the song goes. Less than two years after Patricia moved into her new Habitat house on Meridian Street, she was diagnosed with breast cancer, and within another year she died. God bless you please, Mrs. Robertson, a loving mother, a loyal friend, a trustworthy borrower, a faithful servant.

Habitat has a cure for "lonely eyes" and a lonely nation. Millard called it "love in the mortar joints." It involves using a tool as simple as a hammer or as small as a pen and putting it to work in the building of houses, hope, and community. You can drive a nail with your hammer or write a check with your pen. You can take all the love you have hidden away and share it with your fellow man.

Every time Judy gets out of her chair these days, she limps, and after standing for an hour or two, her ankle swells. You might think that with her fall and the continuing pain and discomfort, she would find another way to volunteer for Habitat. In the fall of 2003 in New Zealand, working on a house with Charlene and Paki Thompson, Judy was the only woman working on the scaffold at the roof's peak. I took her picture and suggested she get down. She gave me a "Go mind your own business—I'm busy" look.

We all need to be busy building houses for those in need, tending to hunger and disease, taking care of our environment, and praying for peace. I don't know if it will be more blessed for others to give than to receive. I do know that through my work with Habitat at every level, I have received much, much more than I have given. I have been blessed beyond my fondest dreams. Before she died, Patricia Robertson had blessed me with her smile.

12

ENID AND THE A-TEAM

After Manila, I promised to work on Habitat houses whenever and wherever the international board met outside of the United States, but I didn't know what was in store. I did know that following the Manila meeting our board would be gathering in Guatemala in June 1997 and "olé" was the only Spanish word in my vocabulary.

To prepare for house building and the board meeting, Judy and I enrolled in a ten-week conversational Spanish course at Mitchell College in Statesville, North Carolina. I had no problem in college and divinity school with the so-called dead languages, Latin, Greek, and Old Testament Hebrew. Spoken languages were different. Judy still reminds me of the night during my sophomore year at Davidson when I tried to rip my German textbook in half and tossed it across the living room. In fact, the only German phrase I remember is an idiom, "hundes haben alles," which means "all dogs have." I don't know what all dogs have, when they got it, or what they plan to do with it, which probably explains why I did not excel at German.

After two ten-week courses of conversational Spanish, I could ask directions to the bathroom, tell someone that I spoke little Spanish, and ask about someone's English. Judy and I together could order a beer and a meal in a restaurant and maybe read a road sign. Beyond this we were lost. That's why our daughter Rachel, who is fluent in Spanish, got a free trip to

Guatemala. Rachel, who studied Spanish in high school and college, spent a semester in Spain and after college worked in a Hispanic neighborhood in Tucson, Arizona, for ten months.

Judy, Rachel, and I arrived in Guatemala City on Saturday, May 24, 1997, and met the rest of our building team. Ian Hay, an accomplished home builder from New Zealand and a fellow member of Habitat's international board, brought his wife, Diana, and his mother, Enid. Ian's father had died the previous year, and this was Enid's first trip since her husband's death. The fact that Enid was seventy-eight years old and could outwork her younger team members motivated for our team. The Leonards and the Hays were joined by Jim and Mary Beth Irvine and their son, Jimmy, daughters Melissa and Heather and future son-in-law Bryan Boring. Jim, also a fellow board member, was a past president of the National Homebuilders Association and ran his own home-building company in Portland, Oregon. David Williams, then a Habitat senior vice president, and his wife, Martha, and niece Laura Butler, also fluent in Spanish, rounded out our team. Maybe it was because we all thought we were such hot-shot builders or because Enid set such a high standard, that we soon began to call ourselves the A-Team.

On Sunday the A-Team climbed into a van and headed for Xela, Guatemala, and the Xela Occidente affiliate where we would spend the week working on three Habitat houses. Halfway to Xela, our van came around a curve and the driver spotted a roadblock of felled trees lying across the road. It did not look like an official roadblock, and the small band of men standing nearby did not look like an official work crew. Stories of kidnappings ran through my head. Our driver stopped, and one of the workers boarded our van. Not understanding Spanish, I had no clue about the discussion that followed and could only wonder about our fate when our driver was waved forward with the man still in our van. A mile down the road we came to the far side of the roadblock. The worker exited the van, and we went on our way unharmed. Fallen trees block traffic just as well as orange barrels. Relax. Breathe deeply. Everything is going to be okay. With the roadblock behind us, I began to concentrate on the countryside and the incredible farming that covered every steep hillside and valley and the widespread poverty visible in the ribcages of starving dogs and tumbledown houses. I recalled from reading that 80 percent of the population lived on subsistence farming and had little economic hope for their future. And I wondered why I had been born in America and not in Guatemala.

The further west we traveled toward Xela, the higher we climbed. In western Guatemala, mountain peaks range from 5,000 to 7,000 feet. Temperatures would rise into the seventies during the day and drop into the fifties at night. It was an ideal time to be in the country and to work outside building homes. Our accommodation in Xela was a modest hotel with separate rooms and baths and a large open space at the building's center. The A-Team met each morning for breakfast and devotions before climbing into the affiliate's white Toyota truck to be dropped at our various work sites. We ran a little experiment to see how many gringos could fit into the back of that Toyota and topped out at ten.

Judy, Rachel, David Williams, and I worked with four Guatemalan families who were laying blocks for Juan's house. In Guatemala, as in many other countries, a few families are very rich and the rest are very poor. There is not much of a middle class. Therefore, few volunteers. Most families will provide support and assistance for their extended families, but certainly not for strangers or distant neighbors. Habitat in Xela arranges labor by placing as many as four families together. During the construction process these families, including spouses and children, work for a week on one family's house and then load the tools into a wheelbarrow and move to the second family's house. This process continues until all four Habitat houses are completed, usually within two to three months.

We arrived at our work site around 8:00 the first morning. Juan, Airee, Ariel, Veronica, Claudio, Esbie, and their families had been working since 6:00 a.m. After introductions, Rachel interpreted for Judy, David, and me our work assignments, which basically were to carry blocks and to shovel and mix sand, lime, and water to produce mescala. *Mescala* was a new word for me, and one I came to respect before the week passed. It is the mason's call for mortar, and if he has to call for it, you are already behind.

We were building next to Juan's existing house, which was over 150 years old and falling down. Both the kitchen and the latrine were outside, as was the local custom. We were using cement blocks that the Habitat families had made weeks before we came by placing a mixture of sand, lime, and stone in a press provided by Habitat. The footings were poured, and our task for the week was to lay as many blocks as we could for this four-room, 400-square-foot house.

It dawned on me that first day that all the skills required to build Juan's house existed among those Habitat families. They knew the proper amounts of sand, lime, and water for the mortar. They could lay block, square corners, and level their work. They knew when and where to use steel bars for bracing and how to place these bars in the walls. Why were *we* there?

Having worked on several Habitat houses in the United States, it seemed that I brought a certain level of skill and/or knowledge helpful to the building process. Not in Guatemala. These families did not need me, and in fact, because I did not understand their language or their construction techniques, my presence slowed them down. I could carry blocks and shovel sand. So could, and did, their nine- and ten-year-old children.

So in Guatemala I discovered again why we build Habitat houses. When George Bush Sr. lost the election for a second term as president of the United States, political pundits kept saying, "It's the economy, stupid. It's the economy." Well, Paul, for Habitat it's the relationship, stupid. It's the relationship. It's the chance to work with families from another culture and country, to talk, laugh, cry, dance, sing, and pray together.

On Thursday, Juan's older son, Manuel, came to work on his father's house. During the week Manuel drove a bus in Xela, but Wednesday was his day off, so he came to help. Manuel and I found ourselves working together carrying blocks, and as we worked we tried to communicate. Manuel knew about as much English as I knew Spanish. So he tried to speak to me in English, and I attempted to speak Spanish. An independent observer would have gotten a big laugh out of our halting conversation.

This experience made me appreciate the difficulty the non-U.S. members of Habitat's international board of directors must have as we blithely conduct our business in English. I thought about Kun Mo Chung from Seoul, Victor Martinez from Guatemala City, Chantal Hudicourt Ewald from Haiti, Nana Prah from Ghana, and Antonio B. (Sonny) de las Reyes from Manila. Manuel taught me to be a better and more compassionate listener.

But Manuel may have learned something as well. He asked me where I lived, and I told him about North Carolina. He asked me why I had come from so far away and from the United States to help his father build his house. I told him that I came with and because of Habitat for Humanity. But that was not what Manuel was asking. He wanted to know *why* I had come, what motivated me. It seemed as if my presence at his father's house, along with that of all the other volunteers, was an experience too amazing for Manuel to grasp.

A few other amazing things were happening that week as well. Every day at lunch, the old white truck would pick up Judy, Rachel, David, and me and take us over to the house site where Ian, Diana, Enid, Martha, and Laura were working with other families. There we would have lunch together and a brief rest before returning to Juan's house. At this site, the house was further along in the construction process, and on Wednesday Ian and his team were framing the roof. Ian Hay exudes enthusiasm. He brought a New Zealand flag to every board meeting and would wave it to get attention. He also brought a map showing New Zealand at the top of the world rather than the bottom. On this Wednesday at lunch, Ian introduced us to a "roof shout," a New Zealand custom for ensuring that a new roof does not leak. To perform a roof shout, one needs a flag, in this case made from an old cement bag and several beer cans. The homeowner then climbs up onto the roof framing and attaches the flag while everyone else drinks beer and shouts. We performed this ritual almost perfectly the first time, especially the beer part. We did a good job of consuming the pizza too. The only one who had trouble was the homeowner, who was scared to death to be so high off the ground.

Rachel especially enjoyed the roof shout, so much so that when we returned to Juan's house, Rachel was laughing, her eyes dancing, as she began to tell Veronica about the roof shout. Veronica picked up on the concept right away. She told Rachel they were poor and never had pizza or beer. Veronica wanted a party with pizza and beer for the families working on Juan's house. Rachel told Veronica they might be poor, but they were fun to be with and work with and took wonderful care of their children. Veronica said that might be true, but they still wanted a party. Judy and I observed all this chatter back and forth, the laughing and jesting, but had to wait for Rachel to explain what was happening.

When she did, Judy told Rachel we would spring for pizza and soft drinks for everyone at Thursday's lunch, but no beer. The offer was accepted, and on Thursday Ian's team joined us at Juan's house for another big party. Friday morning Judy could not get far from either the bed or the bathroom and did not work. By noon on this last day, our families had gathered their tools and lone wheelbarrow and were preparing to walk one and a half miles to Airee's lot to start on his house. All the walls were at full height, yet Juan's house was not yet finished. The families would be here working again in about a month.

As we stood in the street that last day saying our good-byes, realizing we likely wouldn't see each other again, feelings ran deep. Veronica took my hand and said, "Judy, tell Judy," and with her other hand Veronica touched her heart. "El corazón," she said. My interpretation was, "Tell Judy I hold her in my heart."

It's about relationships, stupid. That's why the A-Team continued to travel and build together, and that is why there is an elementary school in Ghana named after Enid Hay. I'll tell you about that later.

Judy and I did not yet know, while we were in Guatemala, that to honor our work there the board of directors of Our Towns Habitat voted to send to Guatemala 10 percent of the price of every house the affiliate built in Mecklenburg and Iredell counties. Since 1997, that tithe has provided the material for 168 houses in Guatemala and has resulted in several Our Towns work teams building homes with families in Guatemala.

13

A BRICK HOUSE

The longest-running video at Grandma and Papa's house is the *Muppet Classic Theater* rendition of "The Three Little Pigs." For at least two years, our grandson Michael, who is six, and his three-year-old sister Lilly have bounded into our house and immediately asked, "Papa, can we watch the wolf?" In response, I start the video and Michael, Lilly, and I watch and act out the wolf's blowing down the straw and stick houses before being defeated by Sandy Pig and her brick house.

I've seen "The Three Little Pigs" at least one hundred times over the last two years, and I too am captivated by the story just as Michael and Lilly are. I like the part where the wolf, having destroyed the straw and stick houses of Randy and Andy Pig, confronts sister Sandy at the door of her house. "Wow! A brick house," the wolf exclaims, looking at Sandy. "You're not a junior petite yourself," Sandy replies as she slams the door in the wolf's face.

More pointedly for me, this story could be a metaphor about the 1.3 billion people in the world's cities living on the streets, under bridges, in storm pipes, or in houses of thatch and sticks, exposed to the wolflike forces of wind, rain, rats, heat, cold, and robbers. A brick house is for me a symbol of Habitat for Humanity's efforts to work with such families in building simple, decent houses capable of withstanding hurricanes and floods.

Even more important, I now think about the bricks used to build a brick house. This is because early one Wednesday morning in April 1998, Judy and I and the A-Team, including Enid, were in Belfast, Northern Ireland, on a Habitat build. We had gone to Belfast on the way to Espleet, Netherlands, for the spring meeting of Habitat for Humanity's international board. Strange as it may seem, I remember little about that board meeting and almost everything about Belfast.

Our construction supervisor in Belfast was Gerry Crossen. Gerry was in his early forties, a tough-looking and -acting Irish Catholic with a build similar to a brick house. In the course of the week we worked together, Gerry told us his story. As a teenager and young man, Gerry belonged to the Irish Republican Army (IRA). He was a gang leader. Gerry vividly remembers and describes those nights when Protestant gangs torched homes in his neighborhood and he would gather his gang and return the favor. For years, Gerry's life consisted mostly of drinking and fighting, bombing and burning. Bitterness and rage consumed Gerry and threatened his marriage.

One night when he was at another drinking party and in a drunken stupor, a sense of despair and hopelessness overwhelmed Gerry. It was then that he uttered a simple plea: "God, help me!" To Gerry's surprise, a sense of calm and peace came over him. And laughing, he said, "The calm was even there the next morning after I sobered up." That sense of calm and peace took over his life. Gerry sought out the Protestant families he had attacked and hurt. "Took several beatings," Gerry said. But he did not stop trying to make amends.

As construction superintendent for Belfast Habitat, Gerry was leading Habitat's effort to construct eighteen brick homes in Glen Cairn Estates, which were being purchased by Protestant families. I found this set of circumstances—Gerry, former IRA gang leader, building for and with Protestant families—amazing in itself. But then I read about the Shankill Butchers and discovered the historical significance of the Glen Cairn site.

In the late 1970s in Belfast, a Protestant gang named the Shankill Butchers, for nearby Shankill Road, a dividing line between Protestant and Catholic neighborhoods, gained notoriety by kidnapping Catholics, slitting their throats, and dumping their bodies on the grounds of a public housing project later torn down to make way for Glen Cairn Estates.

Even though this killing and bloodletting had happened twenty years earlier, the very week the A-Team was in Belfast, the drywall contractor called to tell Gerry that his laborers, who were Catholic, would not work at Glen Cairn. By chance, this was the same week Northern Ireland was to vote on the 1998 Peace Amendment. Police and military vehicles were everywhere, and especially at Glen Cairn, on that Wednesday when Philip Lader, then the U.S. ambassador to Great Britain, came to work with Habitat.

In the midst of this week of hope, confusion, and fear, Gerry Crossen was a force of calm and strength. Gerry led our early morning devotion that Wednesday before we started work. He had brought with him a plastic grocery bag. As Gerry began to talk with us, he reached into that grocery bag and pulled out a brick. He said, "This brick can be broken in half and used as a weapon to break windows in advance of firebombs." At that moment Gerry cocked his powerful arm as if to throw the brick at us. Releasing his arm and his grip, he then said, "On the other hand, this brick can be used to build the wall of a house." And he pointed to the houses at Glen Cairn where brick walls were being laid. "Used this way," Gerry said, "a brick becomes an instrument of peace and provides hope and security for a family."

How shall we use our bricks? In Belfast, Northern Ireland, the Habitat story is not so much a story of house building as it is a story of reconciliation, of Protestants and Catholics working and building together to overcome centuries of hatred and mistrust. Building houses together is a great alternative to building so-called peace walls to separate Protestant and Catholic neighborhoods and defend against firebombs.

Judy and I returned to Belfast in November 2002. One day before we arrived, a young man in his twenties who happened to be Catholic was found nailed to a wooden fence at the entry to a housing development where Protestants lived. Some claimed he had been caught breaking into cars in the neighborhood. The nails driven through his hands had been bent, making his rescue more difficult. Apparently the daily terror of life in Belfast continued, and the peace process remained in disarray.

The Provisional Government established with the passage of the 1998 Peace Amendment was dissolved by Tony Blair in the fall of 2002. Protestants blamed the slow pace of disarmament by the IRA for their withdrawal from the Provisional Government. In the intervening years, however, it appeared that Northern Ireland's economy had experienced significant growth. Public projects, including a new art museum, were under way in Belfast's city center.

But something else had grown too. The thirty-foot high "peace walls" had been raised higher with sheets of tin and webbed netting, all designed to stop and catch bricks and firebombs. Militaristic symbols and curbs painted orange and green or red, white, and blue indicated whether the neighborhood was defended by the Protestant Militia or the Catholic IRA. But in spite of taller peace walls and the disintegration of the Provisional Government, Belfast seemed both more hopeful and more peaceful than four years before.

While in Belfast, Habitat for Humanity's international board approved four new countries, Cambodia, Russia, Panama, and the Republic of Ireland. It was Habitat's work in Northern Ireland and Belfast that paved the way for the work in the Republic of Ireland. It was one of my roles as board chair to travel to Dublin from Belfast, announcing the board's approval of the work in the Republic of Ireland and celebrating the start of Habitat there. The government of the Irish Republic fully supported and welcomed Habitat's presence in their country. After afternoon tea with the republic's president, Mary McAleese, I understood why.

President McAleese, raised as a Catholic, had grown up in Belfast. When she was eight or nine years old, her family's home was invaded by armed men, and the family was forced to leave and abandon their home. She told of days of homelessness ending only when the family was given shelter by nuns. The night before our afternoon tea, the president experienced what had been a reoccurring nightmare, finding herself in a freefall with no place to land. President McAleese did not need to be convinced of the importance of Habitat. She knew better than the rest of us in the room what it is like to live in the midst of terror and to have no home.

On September 11, 2001, when terror came to America, I was in Indianapolis, Indiana, where Habitat volunteers were gathering for the twenty-fifth anniversary of Habitat for Humanity and the celebration of the 100,000th house built by Habitat since its founding in 1976. My role that day was to chair a meeting of the U.S. Council of Habitat, which oversees Habitat's work in the United States. When we received word in midmorning that the planes had hit the twin towers, we prayed and continued the meeting. At the same time, Millard Fuller and his staff made the decision to continue with the twenty-fifth anniversary, a week-long event with seminars, speakers, and celebration.

Many of the attendees were international volunteers and staff from Africa, India, Latin America, and Europe. As the gravity of the terror strike hit home with us, our international friends gathered us in their arms and prayers. What was most comforting to me was the expression of love and concern from those who lived with terror daily, whether from Belfast, Ivory Coast, or Liberia. These were people who understood better than most the new reality being visited upon our America, a reality that was not going away.

What was also uplifting for me was the music of Wintley Phipps, an African-American singer with a voice as deep as the Atlantic Ocean. Wintley, who sang and raised funds for the children of prisoners, was a Habitat supporter because his sister owned a Habitat house and he had seen the change it made in her life. Wintley did not tell us until after he had sung "Heal Our Land" and "I'm Goin' to Pray for This Land" that the songs had been written by Orrin Hatch, the Republican senator from Utah. But that fact is no more astounding than "Amazing Grace" having been written by the captain of a slave ship. The politics of the songwriters didn't concern Wintley. He cared about the songs' messages and meanings, and with a deep and passionate voice he raised our spirits.

It was after I returned from Indianapolis with Wintley Phipps's CD titled *Heal Our Land* that I discovered the song "Too Many Saviors," written by Richard Harris and recorded by Wintley Phipps. That piece took me back to the terror of Belfast and made me think more deeply about the consequences of Homeland Security and the American anti-terror campaign. In the song, it was God's condemnation of each side in Northern Ireland that claimed to fight under his banner that caught my attention. From Harris's perspective, God has no interest in war or the politics that surround it. His first and abiding interest is peace and the well-being of all of people.

What shall we do with our bricks?

14

I REMEMBER HOUSTON

Judy and I had to hurry home from Belfast and the 1998 spring board meeting in Elspeet, Netherlands. We had another commitment as sponsors of a Habitat house in a Jimmy Carter Work Project.

Today, most Carolinians remember Houston and Super Bowl XXXVIII in 2003. We remember the miracle that almost happened when the unsung and unheralded Carolina Panthers met the proven and experienced New England Patriots in America's most hyped sporting event. We remember every pass and touchdown. We remember the tied score with one minute and eight seconds remaining. We remember just two years earlier a season with one win and fifteen losses. We remember the games in 2003 won in waning seconds, and we hoped for just one more miracle in that Super Bowl, but it did not come. To the Panthers' credit they were not satisfied with second place and took little pride in what for most viewers was a great and exciting game.

I remember Houston for another reason. Before the Panthers made their Houston trip, Paul and Judy Leonard and twenty-odd friends were drawn to Houston by Jimmy Carter's challenge. Build one hundred homes in five days. The work project bore his name. We were assigned 2202 Sakowitz. Like the Panthers, I believe in winning.

The goals were clear. Frame and dry-in the house on Monday. Drywall, roof, and side the house on Tuesday. Complete siding and roofing on Wednesday. Install interior trim, doors, and cabinets, and paint on Thursday. Landscape and dedicate on Friday. Piece of cake!

We cheated. On Saturday and Sunday my crew leaders measured the pre-built wall panels and aligned and drilled new holes for the foundation bolts. We also sweated and got a foretaste of the week ahead as temperatures became oppressive by 10:00 a.m. By Sunday noon, the size and scope of our challenge became apparent. Building a house in five days was one challenge. Building a house in five days in 100-degree temperatures was totally different!

Our motley crew was evenly divided between male and female, young and not so young. Most were experienced Habitat volunteers. For a few, this was their first house. At dawn on Monday, Bert Green in his devotion suggested that we dedicate our work for the week to someone in our individual life journeys who had sustained and supported us.

By Monday at 3:00 p.m., we couldn't remember our own names, much less the name of a mentor. In the heat, the medical tent claimed over one hundred workers the first day. Our son Jon had to check in at the first-aid station but was able to return to work. Glenda Helms, the water angel, delivered us from the heat devil on Monday and throughout the week. Every thirty minutes Glenda put a cool bottle of water in your hand and made you drink it, asking the most critical and personal question, "Have you peed?"

Monday took away our pride. When we left the site at 6:30 p.m., our house was not dried in. The trusses were in place, but without roof sheathing and felt. President Carter had said on Sunday night that no one would leave the site on Monday until all houses were dried in. We left, and only President Carter's house was ready. Monday afternoon seemed as if we were both watching and acting in a slow-motion movie. Our minds were willing, but our bodies would not move.

Tuesday was a different story. Our youngsters jumped on the roof and installed plywood and felt by 11:00 a.m. Technically, by then we were only four hours behind schedule. Physically, we were running out of gas. Then the second angel appeared and asked where we needed help. "Roofers," I replied. Within twenty minutes, a skilled six-man crew of roofers was on our roof, and within three hours the roof was completed. Meanwhile, siding was under way on all four walls of the house. The plumbing and electrical subs had completed their "rough-ins" and passed inspections. This was the good news. The bad news was that the heating, ventilation, and air-conditioning (HVAC) subcontractor was nowhere in sight. Work on the interior stopped. No HVAC. No insulation. No drywall.

You guessed it—the third angel. Our problems were not unique. The HVAC subs had pulled off the job Monday night because the houses were not ready, and no one knew when they might return. The project leaders went on radio and TV seeking HVAC subs. The entire project was threatened. I was standing next to one of the project leaders when Charles Simms with Beltway Mechanical walked up. Charles had heard the plea and had come to offer his help. Two crews were on the way. Yes! Charles brought his first crew to 2202 Sakowitz, and by 5:00 p.m. we called the inspector and began insulating the walls. When we left Tuesday, the house was ready for drywall, the siding was 70 percent complete, and the roofing was 100 percent complete. Pride was back. The schedule, however, called for drywall to be complete, and our drywall had not begun. But compared to the surrounding houses, ours was in good shape.

On Wednesday, Ron Bishop's thought for the day was that God would test us but not give us more than we could handle—no matter how hot the day. While most of the crew worked to complete the siding and soffit, a few of us started stocking the drywall. Our drywall crew leader was getting organized when professional drywall hangers came in the front door. Someone has said that luck happens when preparation and opportunity meet. Thanks to the steady pace of our motley crew, 2202 Sakowitz was ready for drywall when the drywallers needed a place to start. Coincidence, or house angel at work? We adopted the roofers, drywallers, plumbers, electricians, HVAC installers, everyone. We gave them water, shirts, and materials. They accepted us and checked on us even after completing their work.

As soon as the drywall was hung, the finishers started. All day Wednesday our crew worked outside and finished the siding. By then, many of us had worked with Linda Cleveland, our homeowner. Linda had four children who would live in this home and supported them through her job as a nursing assistant at a local hospital. She had earned three hundred hours of sweat equity and helped build all the wall panels we used in her home. She was using a week's vacation to work with us and complete her house.

Jimmy Carter said most of the homeowners probably didn't believe on Sunday night that their homes would be completed on Friday. They had been victims of many broken promises. This ultimately was true of

Linda. She didn't really smile until Wednesday. That was when she began to believe that this might really happen, that all the hours she had invested might finally pay off. She smiled when she told me she liked the siding color. She smiled when we asked her opinion about attic stairs and kitchen cabinets. Slowly we were overcoming the social and racial walls that separated us.

Wednesday was hump day. It was also the day that Harry Smith of CBS News visited the Sakowitz site. Thirty-four homes were being built at Sakowitz. I do not know why Harry visited 2202 that day. Elizabeth Leonard, my daughter-in-law, saw him and asked, "Don't I know you?" He told Elizabeth who he was and asked about our house. The next thing I knew, Harry wanted to know why we had come from North Carolina to build houses in 100-degree heat in Houston. He could not understand why twenty-three people would give up their vacations and pay their own way to Houston to build a home. I told him we all had infectious habititus, that we liked working together, that we received more than we gave. I'm not sure he believed any of this. He kept asking why. But he came back with his film crew, and we made the *CBS Evening News* on Friday.

In response to Harry's question, "Why are you doing this?" Kevin Strawn said, "I would do anything for my friend Paul." At Thursday morning's devotion, Kevin had reminded us that all of us were friends and that the standard Jesus set for us was to do anything for our friends. Kevin hoped his motivation for coming to Houston was to follow in the steps of the One who befriends all humankind and calls us to be friends to each other—even, if needed, laying down our lives for each other. Harry Smith should have spent more time with Kevin.

Thursday was paint day. If you stood still inside the house, you were painted. In four hours we applied two coats of paint on walls and ceilings and readied the house for the carpet and tile layers. There was another coincidence. Just as Bob Dobbins and Herb Klippel put the first nail in the first piece of interior window trim, the Andersen window technician visited 2202 Sakowitz and provided instructions that prevented potential errors. Once the carpet folks appeared, we were out of the house again for more than five hours. Some of our crew went to help with other houses, and a few were encouraged to leave early. Late Thursday we got back into the house and started hanging doors and installing baseboards.

Friday was chaos. Some worked outside, planting trees and shrubs and laying sod. Others worked inside to finish the trim, hang kitchen and bath cabinets, install tops, and touch up paint. In our midst, the plumbers, electricians, and HVAC mechanics were trimming out their work, lights, switches, fans, toilets, sinks, vent covers, and so on.

Friday was the day Rosalynn Carter stopped by with a letter from President Carter for the house leader, me. The letter directed me to put down plastic to protect the homeowner's carpets. Early that morning, around 4:00 a.m., President Carter had inspected the thirty-four houses at the site, and mine came up short. The president didn't appreciate just how happy I was to have the carpet in place and the prospect of finishing on time.

Friday was the day we met Sammie, Terence, Brandon, and Niketa, four of Linda's five children. Friday was dedication day. Friday was the day several of our crew left Houston. Friday was chaos and Christmas wrapped together.

It was Christmas for me when ten-year-old Brandon sang "Moving on Up," the theme song from the TV program *The Jeffersons*. The best line was, "We've finally got a piece of the pie."

It was Christmas for me when Linda thanked us and told us how nervous and frightened she'd been on Monday. She feared not knowing what to do or how to help. But she said everyone treated her with respect. "You asked my opinions," she said. "You showed me how to do stuff without talking down to me. You made me feel important."

It was Christmas for me when seven-year-old Niketa came up beside me and looked into the window and said, her face beaming, "That's my room! May I go in and work? I want to help." Once inside, Niketa assured Judy that she could do more than clean up since she painted at school.

Words cannot describe those moments or the feeling that welled up inside, making all the week's work and sweat seem so insignificant beside the hope and happiness that danced in the eyes of these children.

Harry Smith, that is why twenty-three North Carolina friends came to Houston. That is why seven of us stayed Saturday after the dedication to finish cleaning, painting, and installing trim.

And there was one more angel. Actually, it was the same angel with a second act. Remember Charles, the HVAC subcontractor? He returned Friday with his wife, Volena, his daughter, Monica, and his uncle, Ralph. They finished their work and by 5:00 p.m. Friday we had air-conditioning. That in itself was miracle enough on another 100-degree day. But Charles and his family did more. After we had left the site on Friday for the "Habitation Celebration," Charles, Ralph, Volena, and Monica finished the landscaping, laying the remaining sod and cleaning the drive and walks—a job that definitely wasn't in his contract.

As we drove to the house Saturday morning, my first thought was how in the world Judy, Herb, Norma, Leon, Doug, Roberta, and I would finish the inside and also have time to put down the rest of the sod and plant the remaining shrubs. You see, I still didn't understand how God works or believe in angels or believe what Ron said on Wednesday morning. God does indeed provide, for without his angels we might still be working in Houston at 2202 Sakowitz.

15

WILLIE

Millard Fuller had told everyone that going to the Jimmy Carter Work Project in Houston in June would be a religious experience. By that, he meant if you went to Houston in June, you definitely would not want to go to hell.

North Carolina has some Houston-like days in the summer, very hot and very humid. On one of those days after returning from Houston, I had on my house leader hat and we were starting a Habitat house sponsored by the First Presbyterian Church of Mooresville, North Carolina, where Judy and I were members. The Bible offers a lot of advice about building on solid ground, so you would expect a church-sponsored house to get off to a good start. Maybe that was Willie's role. Not Willie Nelson, my country music idol, but Willie the concrete truck driver.

Willie and I met on a hot Thursday afternoon. During the week footings were dug, inspected, and made ready for concrete. Willie delivered the concrete. Willie arrived thirty-five minutes ahead of schedule and way ahead of my coworkers, but this didn't bother Willie. He climbed down from his truck, walked around the ditches, and shook his head, wondering how he could maneuver the giant truck into the small backyard. Within a few minutes, Willie had his plan. He didn't care that others were coming to help. He said, "Don't worry. You and I can do it."

I was thinking, "No way in hell."

With that, Willie jumped in the truck and drove onto the lot. Soon, concrete was rushing down the truck's chute into the footing. With a flat shovel I tried to spread and level the heavy gray mixture of rocks, sand, and cement.

"Don't you have a rake?" Willie asked.

"No, I only brought the shovel."

Willie backed the truck up the hill, expertly filling the footing as the truck moved. I was struggling, sweating and barely keeping up with Willie and the truck. Then Willie motioned for me to come to the truck.

"This batch of concrete is too stiff to move with that shovel," he said. "Let's fill the rest of the bulkheads. Then I'll add some water and it will be easier for you. I take care of my elves."

That was the first time I realized that I was an elf and that Willie was running this operation. And he did run it! He moved the truck as if it were a baby stroller. He placed the concrete exactly where it belonged. By the time the other volunteers arrived, Willie and I had completed two-thirds of the job. The truck was not able to reach two pier footings in the center of the house. Willie did everything to move his truck and minimize the distance required to push the wheelbarrow filled with concrete. For a second time, Willie said, "I take care of my elves."

Let me tell you this: I would be an elf for Willie any day. He knew how to run that concrete truck. More than that, he knew how to take care of his people. He knew that success on the job required teamwork. He knew that his skill in maneuvering the truck could take a load off others. He knew that with the proper balance between man and machine, he could complete a concrete pour accurately and quickly.

He did not stop that day until we were completely satisfied. He moved the truck more than once to be sure the low spots were leveled with more concrete.

Willie will always be one of my heroes. He is a role model. He is a caretaker for everyone around him, and he does what he can to lighten their load. The world needs more Willies. We need more people who look out for others. We need more people who are confident in their skills and abilities and are willing to share their knowledge. We need more people with a can-do attitude.

Many things made no difference that Thursday. It made no difference that I was the builder and Willie was the truck driver. It made no difference that I was white and Willie was black. It made no difference that we knew nothing about each other before we met. Willie and I found common ground in the work we did together. And for a few moments, I had the honor and privilege of being one of Willie's elves.

My experience that Thursday came as close as one can come to uncovering Habitat's secret. Willie and I bypassed the social, racial, and economic barriers our society has built, and for an hour or so on a hot and humid Thursday afternoon, we were one. If you volunteer and work on a Habitat build on any day, in any place, you are likely to have a similar experience.

But if you are smart, you will volunteer on a spring day or a fall day after the footings are poured and the foundation is in place. Otherwise, you might get an unwelcome taste of hell.

16

SAM

The wind had driven away the rain and clouds, but the morning sun did little to warm the day. Judy and I were visiting a few selected Pennsylvania Habitat affiliates and were in West Philly, in the 4900 block of Stiles Street, a narrow street between two-story brick row houses. This was Habitat country or, more modestly, Habitat's block, claimed and rehabilitated over thirteen years. Eighteen houses slowly, carefully, patiently acquired, joyfully and faithfully restored. Eighteen houses built at the turn of the century, owned and occupied then by working families of Irish and Italian descent. Eighteen houses after World War II redlined by lenders, run down by absentee landlords and uncaring tenants, abandoned to drugs, crime, urban sprawl, and homeless squatters. We were standing in the doorway of Habitat's latest rehab on Stiles Street. Members of a church youth group were scraping up the old floor tile. That's when Sheldon Rich, Habitat's executive director, told us about Sam.

Sam formerly had lived in this house. More accurately Sam had squatted in this house. Sam had not owned it. Sam had not paid rent. Sam simply had claimed the house one day by tearing the plywood from a boarded window and moving in.

Soon Sam had developed a routine. He became the neighborhood watchman, sitting on the front stoop or in the upstairs front room. With almost no furniture and a scant food supply, Sam had subsisted on Stiles Street for a number of years.

The Habitat families and staff who lived and worked nearby knew that every winter Sam would be wandering on the street, suffering with hypothermia and/or hunger. Every time a neighbor had found Sam in that condition, the neighbor had taken him to the clinic, prepared warm meals for him, and nursed him back to health.

After Sam had returned to his home, his condition would deteriorate slowly, and then he would be back in the clinic again. The back wall of Sam's house had no siding, and the cold Philadelphia winter easily filled the front room where Sam slept. The neighbors grew weary of Sam's endless cycle of sickness and hunger.

One winter day, after hypothermia and hunger had struck again, a couple of neighbors took Sam to the hospital for an extended stay. That was the day Habitat volunteers had entered Sam's home to rebuild the back wall. That was the day Habitat volunteers had discovered, among bags and bags of garbage and debris, hundreds of dollar bills and unopened checks from the Veterans Administration, Social Security, and former employers. To their amazement, the found money and checks totaled over $20,000.

Habitat volunteers cleaned out Sam's house. They repaired the back wall. The West Philly Habitat affiliate opened two bank accounts in Sam's name and waited for Sam's return, knowing how angry he would be because Habitat and its volunteers had violated his privacy.

Indeed Sam was angry. He did not appreciate the clean house or the newly sided and insulated back wall. He had a deep suspicion of banks and legal documents. He would not sign the papers making his bank accounts official.

Sam died a few weeks after returning from the hospital. Habitat, holding $20,000 of Sam's money, set out to find his teenaged children to tell them of their inheritance.

This is not a typical Habitat story. Most Habitat stories have a more uplifting ending. Most Habitat stories involve mortgage payments, sweat equity, a hand up, not a handout—and tears of joy at the house dedication.

But Sam had not been a Habitat homeowner. He had been a homeless squatter adopted by Habitat families, volunteers, and staff. Sam had been an unwilling partner in the winterizing of his squatter's quarters. Sam had not recognized the conventional ways of handling money. During Sam's days on Stiles Street, an extended family of Habitat neighbors, volunteers, and staff, who were not afraid to hold his hand and call him brother, had cared for him.

Who was Sam? I wanted to know more about him. Maybe he was a Vietnam veteran. Some suggest that almost 30 percent of the homeless once served in our armed forces. Sam could have been an addict to drugs or alcohol or both. Sam was somebody's son and grandson.

When I had the joy of rocking my two-year-old grandson, Sam Davis Leonard, to sleep one night, Sam from West Philly crossed my mind along with the question, could my Sam ever face a similar fate?

Unfortunately, in many ways Sam's plight symbolizes that of 1.3 billion people in this world beyond the reach of Habitat and other housing programs. He needed a simple, decent place to live. He also needed help with health care, counseling, and job training—needs that his neighbors and friends could not provide and that our society increasingly ignores.

Nevertheless, Sam had been fortunate at least to live on Stiles Street and to die among friends who had cared for him.

Habitat currently completes a house somewhere in the world every twenty-four minutes. How many Sams and Sallys die somewhere in the world every twenty-four minutes, waiting for someone to care?

17

CAN WE SING?

It was summer, late on a Wednesday afternoon. The sun was setting over Lake Norman as I sat in the grass with a group of Habitat volunteers. They had come from Indiana to North Carolina on one of their many mission trips. The group was from the New Hope Christian Church and consisted mostly of young adults and a few older leaders. They had arrived in Davidson on the previous Saturday morning after driving all night, bringing tools, cooks, sleeping bags, and plenty of energy. Their home in Davidson was the youth house at Davidson College Presbyterian Church. Their mission was to build a house in partnership with Our Towns Habitat and Lisa Hunt, the homeowner Our Towns had selected.

Lisa had taken the week off and since Monday, with the rest of the group, had been hard at work standing walls, erecting trusses, sheathing the roof, and hanging drywall. In just three workdays, this group had completed 95 percent of the exterior and 75 percent of the interior. That Wednesday evening it was time for a midweek celebration, with dinner and thanksgiving for the week's progress and challenges. It had been my privilege to be the house leader for these dedicated and talented volunteers.

We had hamburgers and hot dogs at the Davidson College Lake Campus and joined together on the grass to sing and give thanks. Other

Habitat families and volunteers joined us. Mark and Aaron played their guitars and led the group songs. Then it happened.

Niko Hunt, Lisa's six-year-old son, soon to be an occupant of the new house, walked up to Mark and Aaron and whispered, "Can we sing 'Jesus Loves the Little Children'?"

Aaron said, "Sure. Will you lead us?"

Niko sat down between Mark and Aaron, and we sang the song with all our hearts:

Jesus loves the little children, all the children of the world.
Red and yellow, black and white, they are precious in his sight.
Jesus loves the little children of the world.

As many times as I had sung "Jesus Loves the Little Children," it had never sounded richer or been more moving and powerful. The Bible says, "A little child shall lead them" (Isaiah 11:6). Niko led us.

The reason that group sang so beautifully that night was that all week long they had been loving Niko and his brother, Nakota, by working with their mother to build a simple, decent place for those boys to live. Their work had given spirit to their song.

Later that night I thought about all the Nikos and Nakotas in the world and how much loving and singing are yet needed in Africa, in India, in Latin America. Millard Fuller, Habitat's founder, kept reminding us that Habitat is not running a lottery for a few lucky families and children. His vision is to see that every child has a safe and decent place to sleep at night.

I know now *who* motivated Niko to request that song. Our Towns Habitat had planned what we called a "Dream Dinner" to raise money to build more houses. Never in the history of humankind had more care, thought, planning, and attention to detail gone into a fund-raising dinner. The volunteers had planned and rehearsed every aspect, including napkin colors and tent cards. The night of the dinner, the Mooresville Citizen Center had never looked so lovingly adorned. But it was Niko and Nakota's mother, Lisa, who stole the show. Lisa is a Native American. Lisa is a warrior. Lisa is a dreamer. Lisa is a messenger. This was her message: "I truly believe that God provides all the blessings, because he says that all good and perfect gifts come from the Father above. But he has to have a willing vessel. You are that vessel. I call you my 'blessing keepers.' God provides the blessings, but you provide the way for his blessings."

"Blessing keepers." What a beautiful and frightening charge. Here's the scary part: What if Lisa is right and we collectively and individually are indeed the keepers of God's blessings? Moreover, what if we keep those blessings for ourselves and refuse or are reluctant to share them? What if we bury our talents? What if we refuse to be his hands and feet? What happens to God's blessings then? And what happens to those for whom God's blessings are intended?

We do not have to guess the answers to these questions. Whether it is Afghanistan or Belfast, New York or Charlotte, we can see in every place the consequences of blessings withheld. We can look into the eyes of the homeless. We can touch the face of an abused and neglected child. We can listen to the angry voices of prisoners and derelicts. We can taste the bitterness of divorced and broken families. We can feel the desperation of addicts, whatever their addiction—money, drugs, sex, or power.

If we are indeed God's blessing keepers, every one of us has the gifts of blessing this world needs. We can share love. We can listen. We can hug. We can hold. We can share food, knowledge, money, power, prayers. We can share every blessing God gives to us.

But is there not a subtler consequence of blessings withheld? Are blessings withheld lost? Can blessing keepers become blessing losers? We see it in a fig tree, withered. We feel it in a spirit, extinguished. We know it in fear, overpowering. We grasp it in emptiness, overwhelming.

This is why Lisa's message was at the same time beautiful and frightening, exciting and disquieting. What a wonderful, amazing power God has given us to be his blessing keepers. What an awesome, humbling responsibility God has given us to be his blessing keepers. If we hold the blessing, we lose it. If we share the blessing, it grows and returns to us tenfold.

Our reason says, "Keep the blessings; protect yourself and your family." Our culture says, "Keep the blessings; you earned them, you deserve them, you made it on your own." Our fear says, "Keep the blessings; build a wall around your house, city, and country for your protection."

Love says, "Just as you did it to one of the least of these who are members of my family, you did it to me" (Matthew 25:40).

"Blessing keeper" or "blessing loser"? It is a choice we have and a choice we make every day.

So you see, Niko, in requesting "Jesus Loves the Little Children," was just following in the footsteps of his mom.

Go, Lisa!

18

AFRICA

A Safari

We went to Africa the first time to photograph animals, not to build Habitat houses. In 1997 Judy and I were debating about a trip to Churchill, Manitoba, to see polar bears when we visited the North Carolina Zoo and learned about a photo safari to Kenya and Tanzania. Per animal, the big five—lion, leopard, elephant, rhinoceros, and cape buffalo—made an African trip a lot less expensive than going to Churchill to see a polar bear. In addition, the photo safari was being sponsored by Charlotte's Discovery Place and Nature Museum, so we probably would have some friends on the trip. We also knew our daughter Amy had spent a semester during her junior year in Kenya, and we thought this might be an opportunity to connect with her experiences. So Africa it was.

We were quite excited when the time for the trip arrived. I had two 35mm cameras and a ton of film. We obtained our brown carry-on bags and green tags from Park East Tours in New York and were ready to go. It seemed a little strange that no one with brown carry-on bags and green tags boarded our Northwest flight from Charlotte to Detroit. We began to question our theory about Charlotte friends joining the safari. Not to worry, we thought. They will appear in Detroit. No brown bags or green tags boarded in Detroit, and not even in Amsterdam, where we caught the KLM flight to Nairobi. In fact, there were no brown bags or green tags in Nairobi, because Judy and I were the only two people in the entire universe going on this safari.

John, our Park East tour guide, who met our KLM flight, explained that the recent violent antigovernment demonstrations in Nairobi and Mombassa resulted in thirteen last-minute tour cancellations. I do not know what was going through Judy's mind, but I was thinking about a return flight. John told us not to worry. Park East was conducting other tours, and the company would run this tour just for the two of us. John's encouragement was somewhat calming, so we decided to sleep on it and make a final decision the next morning on whether to continue.

One headline in the morning Nairobi paper read, "Fifteen Massacred in Mombassa." Beneath the headline was a story of rioting and looting. At breakfast, John reassured us that the violence was isolated in a few cities, that our tour would not be near these places, and that we would be perfectly safe. Because my wife is braver than I am, we stayed and had the experience of our lifetime. Even though we only passed through Nairobi a few times, the impressions of life and the conditions in this city, contrasted with the Masai Mara, led me to write this reflection.

East Africa:
Pastoral,
primal,
pristine,
Masai Mara,
the world as He created it,
unspoiled,
unspeakably beautiful,
spellbinding!

Choking on fumes,
smothered in garbage,
drowning in poverty,
Nairobi,
the city as we built it,
nauseous,
frightening,
failing.

It would be difficult to exaggerate the sense of wonder instilled by the Kenyan countryside and the magnificent animals that roam its plains and drink from its rivers and lakes. I also could not overstate the care and attention we received from Park East Tours or the pure joy of having an entire van and tour guide to ourselves throughout the tour. If we wanted to stop for pictures, we stopped. If we wanted to alter the tour, add a site or stay longer in one place, we did it. Over eight days, we visited several game parks, including Masai Mara in western Kenya, where herds of wildebeest were migrating; Ambosili in southern Kenya at the foot of Mount Kilaminjaro; and Tangiere in Tanzania.

We saw lions mating, zebras playing, elephants trumpeting and protecting their young, flamingos dancing, giraffes necking (fighting), a leopard sleeping, cape buffalo grazing, and hippos wading. There was not a sight, smell, or experience I would not relive—including a journey over roads and ruts that could shake a car to pieces at only ten miles per hour; a visit to a Masai house built from cow dung and filled with smoke and flies; and a fascinating encounter with Israel, our Tanzanian guide.

On the fifth day of our safari, we moved from Kenya to Tanzania and changed guides at the border town of Namanga. Now Israel was our driver and guide, and he quickly demonstrated his skill at spotting birds and animals otherwise hidden from our view. On more than one occasion, Judy or I praised his skill at spotting a movement or shape in the distance and recognizing the animal.

"Israel," I asked, "how did you see that jackal?"

"I saw it because it was there," he replied.

I was thinking, "If you say so."

The next day, without field glasses, Israel spotted a leopard lying one hundred yards away on a slight rise perpendicular to the trail. Not only were we impressed, but so were the five other guides who quickly arrived with their passengers.

"Israel, how did you see that leopard?"

"I saw it because it was there."

By now Israel's answer had etched itself into my brain. "I saw it because it was there." What did he mean? He could have said, "I saw it because I'm good," or "I saw it because I'm experienced," or "I saw it because I get paid to see it."

That night, I mentioned to Israel that I was amazed at the way he spotted animals. "What did you mean," I asked, "when you said, 'I saw it because it was there'?"

Israel laughed and shook his head. "I meant, because it was *there*, I saw it. Because it was looking at me, I saw it."

Israel hadn't bragged. He hadn't taken credit for his talent. He simply had recognized and celebrated his unity with the earth and its creatures, as well as his ability to put himself in the leopard's place by knowing its habits.

Descartes' famous dictum, "I think, therefore I am," embodies the rational mind-set of Western civilization. Israel's "I saw it because it was there" expressed oneness in a world not divided into subject and object. Israel and the leopard were one: "I saw him because he looked into my eyes." This was for me a different way of thinking and living.

That conversation with Israel made me think about what it might mean to see something because it was there. On a Habitat trip to Chicago, I had been told that the folks in the suburbs had no concept of the conditions in the inner city because their modern expressways relieved them of the burden of driving through and seeing the inner city. Looking the other way comes easily for me as well. I don't want a homeless child looking into my eyes. I don't want anyone with needs greater than mine looking into my eyes and laying a claim on me. I'm not into seeing it because it's there, because it's looking into my eyes.

It was good that our safari had come to an end. I'm afraid if we had stayed longer, I might have taken home something more than photographs.

Ghana

We called her Nana from Ghana. Nana Prah was a leader of the Ashanti tribe and an active member of Habitat for Humanity's international board for six years. Our second trip to Africa was to Nana's homeland. Judy and I went to build houses with the A-Team and to attend Habitat's May 28, 1999, international board meeting in Elmina, Ghana. Nana was the host for our meeting, the last board meeting she would attend before leaving the board in October of that year.

I remember Nana's bright and colorful gowns and headdresses. But more important, I remember her warm smile and engaging laughter, her love of Habitat and her people. Nana never forgot the families Habitat served or the staff and volunteers who daily performed that service, often at great sacrifice. Nana was a champion of the people, and as chair of the Africa–Middle East subcommittee and chair of our Strategic Planning Committee, she kept our board focused on our basic mission of building houses and loving people. Most of all, as I remember Nana, I thank her for making possible a trip to her Ashanti tribal area and the Habitat community at Baanuase.

I now see Africa not through the lenses of a camera but through the life and experience of Habitat families, and especially of the family of Gladys Antwi. Gladys Antwi resided on the outskirts of Nkenkasu, Ghana. When we were there with our Habitat A-Team, Gladys lived in a Habitat house with her two children, her mother and two younger sisters. The house was four hundred square feet, including three rooms and a porch. Her house also had a small utility building with a latrine, a bathing room, and a storage room. The house had been built with sun-dried mud bricks plastered inside and out with a mixture of cement and sand. It had a cement floor, but no electricity or running water.

When Judy and I arrived, Gladys and her family moved out of the front room of the house to make a place for us. We lived with Gladys and her family for three nights and experienced life in a Habitat village in Africa. Jim and Mary Beth Irvine; Ian, Diana, and Enid Hay; Chantal Hudicourt; a board member from Haiti; and a few staff members who were part of our team had moved in with other families.

The village was named Baanuase. It had no running water and only limited electricity. A shower consisted of a bar of soap and a bucket of cold water. Meals were prepared over an open fire in the side yard. At the time we were there, ninety families, including 243 children, lived in this village. Each house had land for a garden, and the village had enough land for 110 more houses, a market, and a school. The land had been given by the paramount Ashanti chief, who lived in Nkenkasu and presided over the region. In Ghana, the chief's power comes primarily from the land he controls.

The chief had a Habitat sticker on his car and took obvious pride in the Habitat village he helped found. He took Millard Fuller at his word that anyone without a Habitat bumper sticker on his car was living in sin.

The A-Team met with the chief and his entourage on a Saturday afternoon and joined them as they attended celebrations of life for villagers who had died recently. We danced and sang. We paid respects to our ancestors. One of the chief's ministers passed around glasses and a bottle of schnapps. (We had brought the chief the bottle of schnapps as a gift.) He poured schnapps in each glass. I took a sip as instructed and then poured the remains on the ground in remembrance of my ancestors.

On Sunday we worshipped at the Army of the Cross Church and after the service experienced the overwhelming joy of having the choir lead us back to our bus, singing, "We give thanks to God for you."

On Monday we joined fifty homeowners and worked on four houses, laying blocks, attaching roof tiles, starting a foundation, and repairing a wall damaged by recent rains. That afternoon we dedicated four new houses, one of which belonged to a Muslim family. The chief came, and there was dancing and great joy.

Later that evening the chief returned, and we had a final night with a fire under the trees and stars to absorb the meaning of our visit. We had our first informal meeting with the chief, and while we still had to speak to him through a spokesperson, he permitted one of the Habitat staff to represent him. In the conversations that followed, I was struck by the chief's desire to come to America and see snow.

We did something else that night. The A-Team asked about the plans for the school, the site of which we had seen in a tour of the village. There were no plans, only a hope that one day the village would have a school so that the young children would not have to walk more than a mile to the school in Nkenkasu. We asked the Habitat staff and board president if the homeowners would build the school if the A-Team supplied the materials. We asked the chief, through his spokesman, if he could supply teachers and school materials. With affirmative answers from both, the A-Team agreed to provide $12,000 worth of materials for a six-room school with an office and storage space.

When we left Baanuase the next day, Judy headed home to North Carolina to prepare for the wedding of our younger daughter, Rachel. I traveled to Elmina for the board meeting. The meeting broke little new ground for Habitat. We did learn about the loss of $250,000 in a partnership with Shelter Afrique. A staff member from that organization had been accused of embezzling the funds, and it appeared that Habitat would not recover its investment. This loss increased the board's sensitivity to the risks associated with our worldwide operations and sharpened our focus on the policies and procedures governing Habitat outside the United States.

On a brief side trip, a few board members visited an ancient Portuguese coastal fortress where Africans were imprisoned and held for the slave ships sailing to America in the eighteenth century. The views of the coastline from the fort were spectacular. The views of the cells in the fort and the narrow passageway to the slave ships were powerful reminders of man's cruelty to man and of a history that still has a hold on the descendants of African-American slaves.

Since leaving Ghana that May, Judy and I both have carried with us the images of children laughing, dancing, and holding our hands as we walked through the village, no matter the hour of day or night. And we have remembered women carrying water, blocks, wood, or baskets of bread and fruit on their heads. We have thought about the non-Habitat houses in Nkenkasu, with walls and roofs caving in and washing away with each new rain. We have worried about the future of the new Habitat village and its lack of surface water controls and potable water. We have wondered how the information age can find its way to a village without electricity and a school with few books. And we have sensed just a fraction of the Creator's anguish when he looks upon our world with all its disparity.

It is a long way from the Habitat affiliates I know in the United States to the Baanuase affiliate near Nkenkasu, Ghana. But it is the same mission. All of God's children deserve a simple, decent place to lay their heads at night. That's why Habitat International asks that at least 10 percent of every dollar its affiliates receive be donated to its international house-building program. Habitat volunteers and donors living in the United States contribute 92 percent of the funding for Habitat's work throughout the world. Yet neither Habitat nor any other house-building program has made a dent in the surface of the world's housing need.

This story has a reprise. While in Ghana in 1999, the A-Team designated Enid Hay as our queen mother. Enid, then over eighty years old, had built with us in Guatemala, Belfast, and Ghana. As the week ended, Enid let it be known that she thought this would be her last trip with us. We kidded her and continued to admire her perseverance and kindness.

Enid was right. Within five months of returning home to New Zealand, Enid died from a brain tumor. I thought it fitting to remember Enid by naming the school that the A-Team was funding the Enid Hay Memorial School. In February 2001 some members of the A-Team, absent Enid, gathered again in Baanuase and dedicated a beautiful six-room school built by the Habitat families and named for Enid. It was another warm day under the African sun, one filled with songs and dancing and fond memories of our queen mother and hope for the children of this village.

On this trip Judy and I had the privilege of participating in the dedication of the five thousandth Habitat house built in Ghana, and we had the opportunity to inspect the first house built there. Our three-day tour took us to four different affiliates, where we met families, slept in another Habitat home, and joined in wonderful festivities. But our hearts have remained in Baanuase.

South Africa

I was born in Miami, Florida, in 1940. From then until 1976 I did not travel outside of the United States, and 95 percent of my time was spent in Florida, Georgia, and North Carolina. My only non-southern experiences included two years living in Chicago and a trip to Kansas to visit Judy's parents and to travel with them to Yellowstone National Park. As an indicator of how my life had changed, in 2001 during a six-week period Judy and I traveled to Antarctica, South Africa, and Ghana and to Israel and Jordan. We discovered during the trip to Antarctica that we had joined a very select group that had been to all seven continents. Judy has created an expandable banner with patches from all the countries we have visited, and as of 2005 there are fifty patches, some with dates indicating two or three trips. Habitat has been responsible for many of these travel experiences, but not all.

We went to South Africa in 2001 so that I could participate in a Habitat leadership conference for all of the staff serving in twenty-two countries in Africa, as well as in Egypt, Jordan, and Lebanon. Harry Goodall, the area vice president for this region, met our plane, took us to his house for a shower, and escorted us back to the airport for a five-hour flight to Ghana for the dedication of its five thousandth house as well as the dedication of the Enid Hay Memorial School in Baanuase. After a few days in Ghana, we flew back to South Africa for the conference.

Harry Goodall was raised in the Congo, the son of American missionaries. Harry loved Africa almost more than he loved life. Over an extended career with Habitat, he had been our man on the African scene. He spoke several African languages and understood the culture and its many nuances. Harry knew, for example, that we needed to take a bottle of schnapps when we paid our respects to the Ashanti chief in Nkenkasu, Ghana.

When Habitat decided to decentralize its area offices, it was Harry who decided that the Africa–Middle East office should be in Pretoria and who arranged to rent a vacant embassy for that office. Both the location and ambience of that office lent immediate creditability to our work in South Africa.

Harry and his wife, LuAnn, and their son, Harrison, lived in a pleasant house in a somewhat upscale neighborhood in Pretoria that was surrounded by a twelve-foot wall topped with barbed wire. The house itself had iron bars on all the windows, and inside the house an iron-barred door separated the living quarters from the bedrooms. Accompanying these elaborate security measures were two of the largest dogs I have ever seen.

Harry's nice house with its intimidating security system symbolizes for me the social and economic conditions in South Africa. The physical infrastructure of highways, roads, water, sewer, parks, and public facilities in this country is truly impressive and far surpasses any infrastructure development I witnessed on my trips to other African countries. But the social fabric of the country is unraveling. I don't know if this is true, but we heard that 30 percent of the women living in the country had been raped. Carjacking was rampant, and everyone feared having a car break down on the roadside. Road trips were planned to avoid passing through certain towns at night. HIV/AIDS continues to threaten the population, and already some of our Habitat volunteers are worried about the growing numbers of children who have lost both parents to AIDS and about the ability of AIDS-infected Habitat families to repay their mortgages.

This trip to South Africa was hurried and sheltered, partly because of the time taken to visit Ghana, but also because the leadership conference was held at a beautiful and secluded retreat center. We did have a brief opportunity to visit the Orange Farm Township and build for half a day with Citigroup employees—Citigroup is one of the strongest supporters of Habitat in South Africa. But after that we headed for the conference. My primary task at the leadership conference was to bring the attendees up to date on Habitat for Humanity's strategic plan, but more important to listen to them and understand their issues. Unlike most leadership conferences in the United States, the focus of this conference seemed to be development of the habits of correct and timely reporting to the area office, as well as explanations of new programs and strategies the area office was initiating.

In many respects the conference reflected a top-down approach, which complemented Harry's leadership style. But this is also the direction the money flows in Habitat operations outside of the United States: from the top down. Habitat for Humanity International provides most of the funds to operate in these countries, and the area vice presidents call the shots.

The real danger here is that under these conditions and methods of management, Habitat is not likely to develop strong, self-sustaining affiliates in these countries. And if the donations in the United States shrink or are spread too thinly over too many countries, Habitat's international operations are likely to falter. Many international board members, especially those not from the United States, understood these issues and tried to counterbalance Millard's drive to grow Habitat at any cost.

Our second trip to South Africa, in June 2002, had a completely different focus. Judy and I went to visit with local board members and donors in Pretoria and Cape Town and to participate in the Jimmy Carter Work Project in Durban. Because this visit covered almost two weeks, we were able to check the impressions from our earlier trip and deepen our understanding of the issues, all while gaining a greater appreciation for the beauty and wonder of this country and its people.

Harry and his family also hosted our second visit. The plan was for Judy and me to travel with Harry to Cape Town and back and then travel with Harry, LuAnn, and Harrison to Durban and the Jimmy Carter Work Project. The flight to Cape Town took less than two hours, and upon landing and entering this city nestled between a mountain and the sea, we were enthralled by its beauty. We met with volunteers, some of whom were members of the national board of Habitat South Africa, and were very impressed with the commitment, vision, and energy of this group. They were focused on raising funds and using the upcoming Jimmy Carter Work Project to promote Habitat in South Africa. One board member and a volunteer were particularly concerned about AIDS orphans and building a partnership wherein Habitat could provide a building to house ten or twelve children while another social agency provided the foster parents to watch over them. John Stack, the South African board chair and a Methodist minister, was elected to Habitat's international board in 2002 and brought an important perspective and depth to our board.

By far the most moving part of the trip to Cape Town was our visit to a township jammed with tin shacks and people. But Habitat was at work here, and every fifteenth or twentieth house you saw driving through the township looked like a small cathedral with its gabled roof, painted block walls, porch, glass windows, and wooden doors. This was a community where white members from Cape Town churches were building with Habitat. Some of the volunteers told us they never would have come into the township on their own. Habitat had made it possible for them to see a different part of their community and work beside people they never would have spoken to on the street. The one word the board members used to describe their hope for Habitat and for their country was *reconciliation*. It was the same word we had heard in Belfast.

I left Cape Town filled with more hope for Habitat in South Africa than most countries I had visited outside the United States. I saw the strength of their board. I knew their personal commitment to reconciliation and their faith in Habitat as a vehicle to make it happen. I had noticed in the township among all the tin shacks the presence of water, sewer, and paved streets. Unlike Ghana, where there was only farmland, here the basic utilities were already in place, and with just a little help Habitat could rapidly expand its house building. Many of the poorer South Africans qualified for a government housing grant that would cover up to 60 percent of the cost of a Habitat house, and several families had elected to build with Habitat rather than take a government-built house. When I asked one homeowner why he chose to work with Habitat, he smiled and told me that he enjoyed working on his own house and learning how to build it. His response told me that Habitat's formula of no interest, no profit, sweat equity, and volunteer labor worked as well in South Africa as it did in West Philly.

On the flight back to Johannesburg, Harry shared with me his growing concern about the headquarters staff in Americus, his inability to get new staff approved, the delays in processing travel vouchers, and audits of the area office. I listened, and it was apparent that Harry and Habitat were approaching a crossroads. Harry's insistence on autonomy and our headquarters' focus on accountability would lead the future of our programs in Africa and the Middle East down different roads. I told Harry that he had a decision to make that involved living with more control if he remained with Habitat, and that I would support him no matter which decision he made. As it happened, after a few more examples of policy and procedure violations in the area office over the next year, Habitat and Harry mutually parted ways. While I understood all the reasons, it was a sad occasion for me because I really like Harry and enjoy being with him.

I like LuAnn and Harrison just as much as I like Harry, so it was exciting to learn that we would be driving with the family from Pretoria to Durban. The trip gave Judy and me an opportunity to get to know the family better, and it gave me a chance to wrestle with and tickle seven-year-old Harrison, who designed a "Paul-proof house" of pillows and covers to keep me at bay. Two-thirds of the way to Durban, we stopped and spent the night in a quaint bed-and-breakfast named the Granny Mouse House. June in South Africa is the winter season. Afternoon temperatures rise into the sixties, but at night they often drop into the forties. Our room had a fireplace, and that night when we retired for bed, we discovered that when the maid turned down our covers, she also placed hot water bottles under the sheets and lit the fire. We had a taste of good old-fashioned luxury.

Entering Durban from the west is almost as stunning as the views at Cape Town. Gradually our van descended from the hills, and before us lay a modern city with skyscrapers and shops skirting the Indian Ocean. This grand view from the highway obscured some of Durban's more serious challenges. For example, 30 to 40 percent of the population is unemployed, and 50 percent of the local government's general fund is spent on poverty management and criminal justice. Some have suggested that the high rates of unemployment correlate directly with the high rates of crime. The average income per capita in Durban was only 64 percent of that in Johannesburg, and it was estimated that 650,000 individuals reside in Durban's urban slums.

These facts alone were a good reason for President Carter to choose Durban as the site for his 2002 work project. Actually, Habitat had used the Carter project in Durban to motivate its affiliates throughout the Africa–Middle East region. Together the affiliates developed a plan to build 900 houses in the region before the Durban project started, so that the 100 houses built in Durban would complete a 1,000-house build. That's why, when we arrived at the Durban site, we saw that the house numbers started with 900 and rose to 1,000, which was President Carter's house.

On our way to the city on Sunday, the day before the work project was to begin, Harry received a call on his cell phone. Some problems had developed that demanded Harry's attention. The word had spread on the streets of Durban that Habitat was giving away houses, and the registration lines for foreign and in-country work project volunteers at the civic center were inundated with families needing housing. The other problem was that President Carter was headed to inspect the project site, and Harry needed to be there. This call ended our leisurely drive to Durban.

Harry and I dropped Judy, LuAnn, and Harrison at the Holiday Inn, our home for the week, a nice high-rise hotel overlooking the Indian Ocean and rising above our expectations for lodging, given our previous Jimmy Carter Work Project experiences of a tent and cot at Eagle Butte and a dorm room in Houston. We then drove to meet President Carter and take him through the building site. I have never seen a site better prepared for a work project. All the utilities were in, the streets were paved, one hundred foundations and slabs had been poured, and the first course of blocks had been laid. Door frames and scaffolding were in place. No one could have set a better stage for the drama of a one-hundred-house blitz that would be acted out over the next five days. Even the president, who is a tough taskmaster, seemed pleased as he left us and headed to church.

As we entered the site, on my right, just beyond the temporary project offices, there was an old wooden shack. It seemed out of place with all the new streets and houses soon to be built. I walked up to the shack for a closer inspection and learned that it was a display of the typical houses and community that once stood on this site—a former township that had been deliberately torn down during the days of apartheid as the occupants were removed. The City of Durban had given its full cooperation for the amazing transformation that was about to unfold, selling the land to Habitat at a bargain price and assisting with the infrastructure. We were about to right a wrong and bring hope to a place where hope previously had been destroyed.

Harry and I returned to the hotel and had lunch with our wives. Later in the afternoon, we went to the civic center to register for the project, pick up our house assignments, have dinner, and attend the opening ceremony. The registration lines extended outside the civic center and around the block. After waiting in line awhile and observing how slowly it was moving, Harry exercised executive privilege, walked behind the registration desk, and retrieved the house assignments and packages for each of us. The bad news was that by dinner when registration closed, only 1,500 of the 6,000 volunteers had been registered for the project. Everyone was told that registration would continue Monday morning at the project site.

There was further bad news. My house package indicated that I had been selected as a crew leader, which merited a yellow cap and a distinctive name tag. When completing the application for the Durban build, I did not volunteer for any leadership position and was hoping instead just to fill the role of a laborer. It would have been great to just mix mortar and carry cement blocks all week. Judy had fared no better. She too had a yellow hat and had been assigned as a crew leader on another house. Judy said that the only crew she could lead was one that installed vinyl siding, and there was no vinyl siding in this project. The week was definitely going to be interesting, but just how interesting it turned out to be exceeded my worst nightmare.

Habitat house blitzes start early. We were on the build site by 6:30 a.m. Monday, ready for devotions and instructions, and Judy was desperate for coffee, which was in limited supply. I located house number 978 on the site map and, after devotions, walked directly there. Having been the first volunteer to arrive, I anxiously waited for our house leader and my crew. By 7:45 I had been joined by five other volunteers—three women from the local bank that sponsored this house and two men who also sported yellow caps and crew leader name tags appeared. This was the first time any of the women had been on a construction site. One of my fellow crew leaders was a civil engineer, and the other was a do-it-yourself type.

At 8:00 a.m. we were yet to be joined by other volunteers or, more important, a house leader. While we were getting to know each other, construction on the other houses began. That's when I realized the task of being 978's house leader had fallen to me.

Being a house leader was not a new experience for me. Being the house leader of a house with perimeter walls made of cement block, with no house plan and no knowledgeable crew leaders, was a totally new experience and one that almost defeated me. I started by organizing my small and growing crew of volunteers to lay block on the rear and side walls. I demonstrated how to place the mortar and the blocks and to keep the wall straight and level. Given the fact that the only block I had ever laid in my life was in Guatemala, under close supervision, you can imagine the struggle our group had just getting started. More volunteers arrived, but given the circumstances, there was little for them to do.

Then a man coming down the street stopped and asked if we had a mason. I told him no and said we were desperate. He promised to send one, and about thirty minutes later a mason arrived. His first action was to tear down all the blocks we had laid on the rear wall and start over. That was okay with me. At least we had someone who could get us going. And we were falling way behind the other ninety-nine houses.

Thirty minutes later, five South African Indians stood in front of our house. To hear their banter, you would have thought Job's comforters had arrived. At this point, we would have welcomed anyone. They seemed to be deciding whether they would work on house 978 or seek another opportunity.

Their leader said, "It looks like you could use someone who knows what they are doing. We know masonry."

"You have come to the right house," I said.

"Well, it looks like you need a house leader. Your workers obviously don't know how to lay block."

"I am the house leader," I said. "Would you please go over there and show our volunteers what to do?"

They did. They worked almost every day, and thanks to them we completed house 978 on Friday. An angel knew I was in deep trouble, and he had just sent me five teachers from the M. L. Sultan Technicon, a trade school not far from the site.

In appearance, the most striking of the South African Indians had a full white beard and a white kufi (Muslim prayer hat). He laughingly introduced himself to me as A. K. 47. His eyes danced and laughed. "A. K. Mohammed," he said. I laughed too, but I was thinking 9/11. I was thinking terrorist. I was thinking Muslim. I watched A. K. He joined the others and clearly outworked everyone. At lunch, A. K. always took a vegetarian meal. In the afternoon, A. K. told me he had promised to help the women on a house up the street but would come back if I needed him. A. K. came every day that week, working mostly on house 978 but helping other houses as well. On Tuesday and Wednesday, A. K. was hassled by security and might have been turned away from the build except for his ability to take no offense and to keep talking. Every day A. K. followed his diet and took time for prayers.

On Thursday A. K. came an hour late. He told me that a reporter for *Habitat World* had stopped him for an interview. The reporter wanted to know how he as a Muslim felt working on a Christian project. A. K., with tears forming in the corners of his eyes, said, "I told them I did not look at it that way. My religion tells me to care for my neighbors and people in need. That is why I am here. That is why I have been here all week."

Later that same day, A. K. invited Judy and me for dinner at his home on Saturday night after the build. When we said yes, he volunteered to pick us up at our hotel. On Friday A. K. said he would leave before noon to attend prayers at his mosque. And on Saturday evening, true to his word, A. K. called for us at the hotel at 6:00 p.m. On the way to A. K.'s house, I thanked him for his hospitality and the ride. A. K. said, "No bother. My religion teaches me to take care of strangers in my land, and you are a long way from home."

After we reached A. K.'s house, family and friends who had gathered for the evening greeted us. If he had looked, A. K. would have seen the tears forming in the corners of my eyes when he introduced me to his son, Ibrahim, as Uncle Paul.

One other thing happened that Saturday that brought tears to my eyes. In the morning Judy and I had visited the newly completed Habitat community to see the finished houses with their distinctive brass house numbers and Jimmy Carter Work Project plaques. There were no volunteers or workers. It was a day of much-needed rest. I took a few pictures. Then we came to house number 911. There, mounted beside the front door between the number 911 and the Jimmy Carter plaque, was a piece of molten glass provided by Mindy Rosengarten, a volunteer from New York City. Prior to Durban, Mindy had served as a chaplain at Ground Zero, where she had counseled police, firefighters, and morgue workers who pulled bodies from the rubble. This piece of molten glass had been given to Mindy the night before she left for South Africa by one of the officers. It was from the ruins of the twin towers of the World Trade Center.

The officer had told Mindy to take the molten glass to South Africa and find a place where it could symbolize hope for the world's future (*Habichatt*, July 3, 2002).

Habitat House 911 in Durban is a moving symbol of this hope for the future, a hope that was born in the ruins of the World Trade Center.

Judy and I flew home on Sunday. I left South Africa not only with a renewed sense of hope from house 911 but also with a strong sense that I had been helped through house 978 when I was unable to help myself.

19

INDIA

Coffee or Tea?

In the early spring of 1999, after Judy and I had returned from a vacation to Egypt, I received a call from Steve Weir, Habitat's director of our Asia-Pacific region. Steve asked me if I would go to India to evaluate Habitat's program and the capabilities of P. Augustine, the national director of Habitat India. This was a challenging request that required serious thought. First, India was not on the list of places I wanted to visit. Second, we were already scheduled to go to Ghana in May to build with the A-Team in Baanuase and to the international board meeting in Elmina. To top that off, our daughter Rachel's wedding was set for early June at our home.

Fortunately for me and for Steve, I am married to a woman whose motto is "Have passport, will travel." As far as I know, there is no place on earth Judy would not visit, and she could be ready to leave the next day. It would not matter to her if the State Department had issued warnings. Andy, our son and a Charlotte-Mecklenburg police captain, threatened to have her arrested to prevent our trip to Turkey two weeks before the 2003 Iraq war began, but that didn't stop her. So when I told Judy about Steve's request, her only question was, "When do we leave?" and her only requirement was that it had to be after

Rachel's wedding. With Judy by my side, I find it difficult to decline travel and adventure.

So I called Steve and told him we would go to India, and we developed a plan. Steve told me that relationships are important to Indians and that little is accomplished or decided without a trusting relationship. So we decided that Judy and I would host P. Augustine and his wife, Josephine, in our home at Lake Norman for a week in early May. Then in July we would spend a month in India visiting the national office and several Habitat affiliates. At the conclusion of the visit, I would report to Steve with my observations and recommendations.

My first introduction to India and its culture began at the baggage claim in the Charlotte Douglas International Airport. That's where Judy and I greeted Augustine and Josephine, and that's where Josephine collected and carried their luggage as Augustine walked ahead. Seeing what was happening, I offered my help. Josephine refused. I took a bag anyway, and then even Augustine carried one. This scene or a similar one repeated itself many times during the week. I was walking with Augustine and Josephine on Davidson's Main Street, headed for the Soda Shop and a little local cuisine, when I suddenly noticed that Josephine was twenty feet behind us. I stopped and went back for her. Josephine explained that it was customary in her country for the women to walk behind their husbands. I told her that this was America and I wanted her to walk with us. Later, after Judy and I had returned from India, Judy observed that I quite often walked off and left her. After that happened a few times, Judy began calling out, "India!" and I started to think I might like to have an Indian wife.

We took Augustine and Josephine to see Habitat homes built by Our Towns Habitat. They were awed by the size of the 1,050-square-foot homes with three bedrooms and one-and-a-half baths. After we visited with Augustine and Josephine in their home outside of Bangalore, their reaction was more understandable. These Habitat homes were larger than even their personal residence. They were surprised that some of the homeowners were Caucasian, because they believed that the only poor Americans were black. On a visit to Charlotte, Josephine asked where all the people were. Charlotte looked like an abandoned city to her. After we had experienced the mass of humanity pressing against us on the streets of Delhi and Bangalore, her question about Charlotte's empty streets made more sense.

Josephine seemed most at home attending mass at Saint Teresa's Catholic Church in Mooresville. Both Josephine and Augustine were

raised as Catholics. Augustine had even been educated for the priest-
hood. But mass was still central to Josephine's life, and her attendance
at daily mass while she stayed with us gave her something familiar to
hold on to in the midst of a very strange place. Josephine had seldom
traveled beyond their home in Bangalore, even to other parts of India.
America and its culture shocked all of her sensibilities.

If the purpose of Augustine and Josephine's visit was for the couples
to build a comfortable relationship, we succeeded. At breakfast on their
final day with us, Judy asked Augustine and Josephine, "Coffee or tea?"
and they both replied, as they had every morning, "Coffee or tea."
Morning is not Judy's best time of day. I usually don't even attempt conversation until she is well into her second cup of coffee. So the morning
ritual of offering coffee or tea to our guests and not getting a direct
answer had been puzzling and a little frustrating. So Judy asked,
politely, "Why not tell me what you would prefer? We have both!"
Augustine explained that in India hosts might offer guests drinks or
food they did not have. If a guest requested such an item, the host
would run to the store or suffer an unnecessary embarrassment. So the
polite response in Indian society is to say, "We will have what you are
having—coffee or tea."

This discussion itself told us we had established a communication
link we could build upon. But we had no idea of the complex cultural
mores and dress awaiting us in India, or the subtleties of communication. During our visit to the Trichy affiliate, the affiliate president called
soon after Judy and I checked into our hotel. He explained the afternoon's and evening's activities, which included a tour of a nearby Habitat neighborhood and a much longer trip to a Habitat community north
of the city. He further explained that he and the national director,
Augustine, had talked and that the national director had felt the evening
trip would be too much for us; therefore, he had arranged instead for us
to visit a local Hindu temple and skip the evening event. Without thinking, I replied that whatever Augustine thought was best was okay with
us. So after we had completed the afternoon neighborhood tour, I was
surprised when several people wanted to know if we were going north
with them. When we said no, their disappointment was obvious. Then
we were greatly embarrassed the next morning to learn that we had disappointed more than two hundred people who had waited in the community to greet us. I had missed the subtle point: Augustine was offering
a face-saving way out of a rather long and arduous side trip, but it was
not proper to take his offer. We should have gone to the community—

and we would have, without question, if Augustine and the local president had not offered the alternative or if we had understood the offer.

So the next time someone asks, "Coffee or tea?" think long and hard about your answer, especially if you are in India.

A Mouse in the House

It was not just any house the mouse was in. It was Roosevelt House, the home of the U.S. ambassador to India. And it was not just any mouse that was in Roosevelt House, but a mouse that starred in a children's story coauthored by Sam Celeste, the three-year-old son of Ambassador Richard F. Celeste and Sam's mother, Jacqueline Lundquist. Judy and I know Dick, Jacqueline, and Sam because Dick and I served on the international board of Habitat for Humanity during 1996 and 1997. And we know about the mouse in Roosevelt House because during our thirty days in India, we spent four nights there as guests of Dick and Jacqueline.

When someone says, "Come see us," especially when headed for a new country and an important assignment, it's hard to be sure whether this is simply a parting gesture or a true invitation. Once Judy and I knew we were going to India, we e-mailed Dick to tell him about our planned trip. His reply included an invitation to stay at the Roosevelt House on the embassy grounds while we were in Delhi. Judy and I were excited about Dick's invitation, but we left for India not totally clear about the details of getting to the embassy.

Todd Garth, a Habitat employee in Delhi, offered to meet us at the airport and take us to the embassy, where we had planned to spend two nights. As we were leaving the plane's jetway and heading for immigration, a gentleman asked, "Mrs. Leonard?" Judy nodded. He said, "I am Rashid from the embassy. Please come with me, and the ambassador will be here to greet you in a moment." Rashid can meet me at any airport. We breezed through immigration in a matter of moments. As we were waiting for our luggage, Ambassador Celeste showed up in blue jeans and a golf shirt to welcome us to Delhi. As we exited the airport with the ambassador, we found Todd Garth, thanked him for waiting, and told him we wouldn't need a ride to the embassy. By now complete shock set in. As a child I remember sayings like "living high on the hog" or "living in high cotton." When the ambassador met us at the airport and took us in his chauffeured SUV to the embassy, I could feel that cotton, and it seemed really high!

In some ways, spending our first two days in the company of the ambassador, living in his home and among the many household employees ready to serve at any hint of need, was probably not the best introduction to India. On the other hand, this experience provided an invaluable reference point for the rest of our trip.

We had arrived on Friday evening. On Saturday we walked with Dick, Jacqueline, and Sam over the embassy grounds. Dick took us to his present office and to an adjacent office he had occupied from 1963 to 1967 when he served as special assistant to Chester Bowles, then the U.S. ambassador to India.

On Sunday Dick and Jacqueline took us on a tour of Delhi, both old and new. *India*, a guidebook published by Lonely Planet, accurately describes old and new Delhi: "Delhi is the capital of India. . . . The city actually consists of two parts. Old Delhi was the capital of Muslim India between the 17th and 19th centuries. In Old Delhi you will find many mosques, monuments and forts relating to India's Muslim history. . . . New Delhi is the imperial city created as the capital of India by the British. It is a spacious, open city and contains many embassies and government buildings" (7th ed., November 1997, p. 193).

We drove past the ruins of the Red Fort, which had been completed in 1648 at the height of Mughal power. We walked along Chandi Chowk, the main street of old Delhi and a teeming bazaar whose sidewalks were filled with street merchants offering every imaginable item for sale. Back in the car, we rode to Connaught Place in New Delhi and then to Parliament Street (Sansad Marg) to see the salmon-colored observatory constructed by Maharaja Jai Singh II in 1725. We saw the India Gate, a 42-meter-high arch of triumph bearing the names of eighty-five thousand Indian army veterans who died in previous conflicts, including World War I. In the same area we saw Rashtrapati Bhavan, the official residence of the Indian president, and the nearby secretariat and parliamentary buildings constructed during the British era. Along the way, we had the first of many sightings of snake charmers and saw roadside hovels of tarps and tin. In one of my pictures I can count thirty vultures flying overhead, waiting perhaps for the next cow or human to expire. Women holding up supposedly sick or diseased children knocked on the car windows and begged at most intersections.

We returned to Roosevelt House for a swim in the backyard pool, an early dinner, and a chat to catch up on Habitat and on Dick's first year as ambassador. During our stay there, India was at war with Pakistan.

Indian planes were making daily bombing raids, and India's dead soldiers were being celebrated as national heroes. I was surprised that Dick spent so much time with us, for the United States was playing a key role mediating an end to this conflict. Dick had been appointed as ambassador by President Clinton in 1997. He had extensive governmental experience, having served as director of the Peace Corps under President Carter from 1979 to 1981 and for two terms as governor of Ohio from 1983 to 1991. Dick was familiar with crises and always maintained a calm and steady approach to problem solving. He knew how to listen and bargain. I had seen him in action as a member of Habitat's international board.

Late that Sunday evening, Rashid took us to the airport for our flight to Bangalore and Habitat India's national office. But that was not the end of our embassy experience. We left that Sunday with an invitation to return and spend two more days at the end of our trip, which we did. Jacqueline offered to have the embassy staff plan a sightseeing trip to Japuar and an opportunity to see the Agra and the Taj Mahal upon our return to Delhi.

Two weeks later while Judy and I were in Hyderabad, Dick hosted a fund-raising dinner there and invited us to attend. On that occasion I sat beside B. Ramalinga Raju, chairman of Satyam Computers Service, Ltd., and learned that his company employed four hundred people in Bangalore who did nothing but process data for State Farm Insurance Company. Satyam also had contracts with forty Fortune 500 companies, including Bank of America, General Electric, and General Motors. Mr. Raju had never heard of Habitat India and had no concept of its mission, but he asked great questions about repayment rates and house design and costs. Sitting to my left was K. S. Madhaven, managing director of Tecumseh, India, who was interested in discussing housing opportunities Habitat might provide for workers at his plants in Hyderabad and Delhi. It was at that dinner that I understood the wealth and potential of India and realized that Habitat India had no contact with this potent group. Judy received similar insights when we returned to the embassy the second time. She shared lunch with Jacqueline and her several young female friends who were entrepreneurs, including a former Miss India with significant charitable interests and no knowledge of Habitat.

Dick and Jacqueline had provided an exposure to a side of India we otherwise never would have experienced. This exposure proved invaluable to me in my assessment of the Habitat program there and enabled me to see both its potential and failings. U.S. taxpayers will be pleased

to know that during our last day at the Roosevelt House, we met with
the business manager and received a bill for the transportation and services we had received from the embassy staff.

Our final night at Roosevelt House included a small dinner party
with two other couples. One of the gentlemen was Gulshan Grover, the
"bad man" in many Indian movies. Jacqueline introduced Gulshan to
the house staff and their children and he posed for pictures. After dinner, the conversation turned to the India-Pakistan war and the donations that were being solicited for the widows of soldiers. One of the
guests asked if the group thought those widows would ever receive any
of the money. He mentioned a similar charitable drive that had paid out
nothing. I chimed in that I doubted that was possible, because on my
recent visits to the Habitat affiliates in India, I had been impressed with
the very strict audit requirements imposed by the Indian government.
This comment drew a few hearty laughs and the reply that those audits
had been required because Habitat was a foreign corporation and
audits meant nothing. Someone agreed and added that a local government recently presented detailed audited expenses for a $250,000
bridge, but no one had been able to find the bridge. With that everyone
laughed, and the laughter revealed an almost insurmountable wall of
mistrust of government and charity in a country where baksheesh, or
gratuities, small and large, must accompany almost every request for
service. In fact, during the thirty days we were in India, the Habitat
national office was without telephone, e-mail, and fax service for
twenty days because Augustine, acting on principle, refused to tip the
repair man. No tip. No telephone. How could Habitat India, a Christian charity, ever scale that wall of mistrust?

Bangalore and Points South

I hate to admit this, but before planning our trip to India and talking to
our friends, David and Elizabeth Martin, who had lived in Bangalore
briefly, I had never heard of Bangalore. And before we landed in Bangalore, I knew it simply as the site of Habitat India's national office and
the home of Augustine and Josephine. Today many Americans know
about Bangalore because that is where so many American call center
and programmer jobs have gone. Bangalore has many nicknames: Garden City, India's Silicon Valley, Fashion Capital of India, Fruit Market
of the South. It also still goes by the old name, Benda Kalu Ooru, given
to it by the legendary King Veeraballa, who when lost and hungry in the

forest was met by an old woman who gave him baked beans. A loose translation is "place of baked beans."

But Bangalore has moved far beyond its reputation for baked beans. Today it is India's fifth largest city, with a population approaching six million, and is also the fastest-growing city in Asia. It has an 80 percent literacy rate. Type "Bangalore" in Google's search engine, and the hits will astound you: Indian Statistical Institute, Indian Institute of Information Technology, Indian Institute of Management Bangalore, Indian Institute of Science, and Software Technology Parks of India, to mention a few.

When Judy and I landed at the Bangalore airport one hour late on Sunday, July 20, 1999, we were greeted by Augustine and Josephine; their daughters, Zeno, Reni, and Sandi; Josephine's two sisters, Feebi and Merci; her brother Philip; and Lawrence and Edwin from the Habitat national office. Judy and I were amazed at the size of the welcoming party and didn't realize it was an indicator of the great warmth and love with which we would be received everywhere. But, as we managed to do more than once on our visit, we quickly disappointed our hosts. Since the hour was late, we declined dinner, instead inviting everyone to our hotel room so that we could thank them for their warm greeting. They would have preferred our going to dinner, but there was no gesture or sign of their disappointment.

Augustine's disappointment was obvious, however, when he saw our hotel room. Judy and I assured him that the room was fine, but he was not satisfied. He noted that there was no television, which he later said was included in the room rate, and there were water stains on the walls and ceilings. Before the welcoming party left, Lawrence from the Habitat office was assigned to collect us for breakfast. And we discovered when Lawrence arrived the next morning that Augustine had changed our hotel. We enjoyed a delicious English breakfast with Lawrence, and then Augustine appeared with his driver and took us to the national office.

At the national office everyone stood when we entered, and we were greeted with a prayer, given garlands, marked with a tilak (a mark made on the forehead to indicate good omen, happiness, etc.), and sprinkled with water. Staff introduced themselves, and Augustine explained the purpose of our visit. He told them that Judy and I would be meeting with each one individually, and he encouraged them to share openly with us. One assignment that Steve Weir, Habitat's director of Asia Pacific, had given me was to assess Augustine's team. Steve had the impression that Augustine was hiring from India's lower caste, and he sensed that this might be a problem. I had no business accepting this task as part of my assignment, because I could not tell one caste from another and basically did not care. Dress, language, and behaviors all telegraph caste in Indian society, signals missed by most foreigners.

Judy and I spent the next day and a half meeting with Augustine's staff. Each interview lasted sixty to ninety minutes and was conducted on a mutual basis of getting to know each other and sharing insights about the program and challenges facing Habitat India. While the staff included a mix of both experienced and inexperienced persons, I was impressed with the education, energy, commitment, and understanding of all but a few. Pauline, Augustine's administrative manager, had previously worked in banking and for another non-government agency. She had been attracted to Habitat by the opportunity to express her faith through service. Many Habitat employees share this same motivation. They certainly are not motivated by earning potential. Pauline struck me as being bright and capable. She wanted to see Habitat do a better job of linking its financial support to program goals and effectiveness. For example, if an affiliate wanted more money, it should be encouraged to improve the repayment rates for its mortgages. Pauline also emphasized the great need for housing in India and expressed impatience with Habitat's inability to reach more families.

Every interview increased my understanding of Habitat's operations and challenges in India and provided insight about its staff. No one held back. Stanley George, the accountant for international funds, wanted to know when Habitat for Humanity would give him feedback on his reports. He wanted to know how India stood with respect to other countries and what steps he could take to improve and better manage the flow of funds. Sangeetha, a new staff member, wanted to know how the national staff could work with a homeowner family to build a house and what she could do to get Habitat campus chapters started in Bangalore and elsewhere. The longest-term employee, other than Augustine, was Teresa, who told us about the struggle to establish an India national office beginning in 1995. She spoke of the battle to gain cooperation from the existing affiliates and of eighteen-hour days handling communications, coordinating short-term missions, and following up with national and international partners. In short, Teresa had performed all the functions now divided among a much larger staff.

My biggest shock was that the staff of the India national office included a director, a secretary, an administrative assistant, a controller and two assistants, a resource development officer, and an assistant and a driver for Augustine, and the total of all of these salaries was less than $48,000 a year. Judy and I discovered the power of a dollar in India: a motel room on the Indian Ocean, $10 per night; a hotel room in a tiger preserve at an old British hill station, $17 per night, including dinner and breakfast. Apparently many companies in the United States today have discovered this same power as they outsource work to these bright and energetic people.

Since the interviews had given me little insight into the question of caste, later in my travels I mentioned the issue to John Bell, an international partner from the United States, employed by Habitat International to work in India. John's quick reply was that Augustine was not hiring all lower-caste people. He was hiring all Christians, who in India are largely lower caste. In many ways John's observation raised for me the question of how Habitat can maintain a Christian identity and work effectively in a country whose population is only 3 percent Christian and whose economy and resources are controlled mostly by Hindus and Muslims. This issue became even more troubling after I met with Habitat's national board.

But it was not all work in Bangalore. Augustine and Josephine had taken a boat ride on Lake Norman when they visited us, and Augustine wanted us to experience Ulsoor Lake. So after the interviews were concluded Tuesday morning, Augustine, Pauline, Teresa, Sangeetha, and Judy and I set out for a wonderful boat trip on sunny Lake Ulsoor, then cooled off with a visit to the stunning Bangalore Science Museum, with its exhibits on local manufacturing and India's space exploration.

While the boat ride and the museum visit were memorable, this was really our first day traveling through Bangalore, competing for space with ox carts, huge lorries, bicycles laden with packages, motor scooters with four and five passengers, tractors and cows on the crowded streets and highways. I wanted to cover my eyes and forget where I was. But as I watched, it appeared that the traffic had been choreographed by the master of all movement. Collisions that appeared certain to occur were avoided by last-second swerves either right or left or a sudden stop. I am sure I set a record for prayer on Bangalore's streets.

As the day was ending, we stopped in the parking area of the government building that housed the legislature for the state of Karnataka, of which Bangalore is the capital. This building was striking for its setting on a hill overlooking a garden, its size and magnificent architecture, and also for an inscription carved in gold over the building's entry: "Government work is God's work."

Sometimes it's difficult to let go of something you have seen or heard. The inscription over the entry to that legislative building would not go away. Without prompting, a small voice sounded in my head: "Not where I come from! Government's work is the devil's work." I laughed at this thought. I started thinking about the founding of the United States on the principle of separation of church and state and the continual efforts of the religious right and the religious left to influence and control legislation in America. I knew how cynical I had become about our political process and the buying of elections and influence.

"Government's work is God's work." Wow! Is it possible? I asked Augustine about the author of this inscription. "Who wrote it? Where does it come from?" To the best of his knowledge, it came from the Bangalore legislature, the Vidhana Soudha itself. It came from the people who had designed and built this great legislative hall.

I wondered what Ambassador Celeste thought about this inscription and whether he felt his current efforts to abate the Indian and Pakistani fighting involved God's work. I wondered how nervous some of our elected representatives in the United States might become if they considered even for a moment that their work was God's work. I wondered how Americans who believe that "the government which governs least governs best" would react to this inscription. This idea that government's work is God's work would not go away.

Talk about coincidence! The very next morning, June 24, 1999, I picked up the *Times of India* and read the following editorial:

Schooling of God

"We will win this war," asserted a woman before US President Lincoln, during the Civil War, "because God is on our side." But the response from the statesman was, "All we can hope for is that we are on God's side." Not all politicians are quite so modest, and as a class, they feel within their rights to invoke divine support for their own schemes, as if He were a kind of "Cosmic Bell-hop." Bangalore's legislature (known as Vidhana Soudha) carries the crest "Government's work is God's work," in the hope, presumably, that at least some of the divine stardust would rub off on the mortal lawmakers below.

In the US, last week, the House of Representatives debated the shocking incidents of schoolroom mayhem and murder and illegal use of firearms by juveniles. The intense pressure to change laws had come from the parents, educationists and sociologists on the one hand and the resourceful gun lobby on the other. True to their proverbial ambivalence, the lawmakers adopted a resolution to post the Ten Commandments (handed over by God to Moses) in every classroom in the nation. They were swayed by arguments that this display would curb gun-toting and violence. At midnight, the same day, however, the House of Representatives was also swayed by the gun lobby's view that rights of law-abiding citizens would be harmed by going beyond this. So they approved amendments making it easier for people to buy firearms at gun shows and exempted checks for background of gun-buyers.

As Daniel Defoe wrote: "Whenever God erects a house of prayer, the Devil always builds a chapel there. And it will be found on examination that the latter has the greater congregation." It was at Pearl Harbour in December 1941, that Lt. Commander Howell Forgy, doubling as chaplain for an American Cruiser crew, said famously, "Praise the Lord, and pass the ammunition." That was perhaps our century's version of Cromwell's message to his troops, "To trust in God, and keep the (gun) powder dry." But a British survey among churchmen last year revealed that very few "men of God" could recall the Ten Commandments, and a younger respondent even called the emphasis on orders, "negative in nature because they only emphasized what not to do, rather than how to cope with life's dilemmas." (Source: *The Times of India*)

This editorial made it clear that it is not God who needs schooling and that doing what one pleases or thinks is best just might not be God's work. I began to think, yes, government work *could be* God's work. Teaching *could be* God's work. Business, health care, banking, policing, planning, building, waiting—every task one does—*could be* God's work. Every job has the potential to be God's work. Every individual has the opportunity to do God's work. But which individuals or institutions can honestly claim to do God's work? As Daniel Defoe suggested, we all probably spend most of our time in the devil's chapel. Was there a message here for Habitat for Humanity and its claims to be God's ministry, to demonstrate his love through its home-building activities? Is it possible for Habitat for Humanity to avoid assuming that God is on its side? Could it learn to pray always that it be found on God's side?

A bit more modesty in its claims to follow God could pave the way for Habitat for Humanity to develop significant and lasting partnerships with our Hindu and Muslim brethren. Absent such a mind-set, Habitat India and Habitat for Humanity seemed destined to play minor roles in overcoming the housing plight of the poor in many parts of the world.

Is government work God's work? Is Habitat for Humanity God's work? Maybe. It depends.

Hosur and Hyderabad

Before we left Bangalore for Mysour, two more experiences left an impression on our minds and hearts. Josephine and Augustine hosted a dinner at their home in nearby Hosur with their family. The drive there demonstrated the traffic war Augustine and his driver fought every day and reminded us that distance and time do not correlate from country to country. Hosur did provide some relief from the congestion of Bangalore, and I have a wonderful nighttime photograph of the city's lights from a Hindu temple hill overlooking Hosur.

When we arrived at Augustine's house, we were greeted in the small enclosed courtyard by the smiling faces of Josephine; her sisters, Merci and Feebi; and their daughters, Zeno, Sandi, and Reni. Augustine's modest house, with a small living room, office, kitchen, and two bedrooms, provided shelter for six family members. Josephine's sister Merci had lived with them for eight years. We soon learned another lesson about the roles of husbands and wives in India. A table had been set for three places—Judy, me, and Augustine. The young girls sat and ate on the sofa, but Josephine and her sister ate only after we had finished our meal. We asked Josephine to join us, but she declined. Throughout our marriage Judy and I have seen each other as equal partners in all of life's ventures—family, business, church, travel and tragedy. I couldn't conceive of the relationship I was seeing in this home. I also couldn't conceive of the fact that wives are burned, often fatally, in kitchen "accidents" when they have in some way disgraced their husband and his family. I understood better why Josephine had carried Augustine's luggage and walked behind him on Davidson's Main Street.

While we were in Delhi, Jacqueline Lundquist had encouraged Judy to read the personal ads in the *Times of India*. There Judy had discovered page after page of ads seeking or offering women for marriage. The most highly prized seemed to be those of lighter skin who also were convent educated, which seemed like an odd advantage in a Hindu country. During our visit at Augustine's, we also learned that he was seeking marriage proposals for Merci, Josephine's sister. If one of my sister-in-laws had been living with me for eight years, I would have been seeking a proposal as well, and most any offer would have been accepted. But Augustine's role was simply to vet the offers from the marriage brokers and pass them to Merci's father for a final decision. We wondered what role Merci might have in that decision, since she was a well-educated school teacher supporting herself. In fact, within a week, Augustine had been approached by two marriage brokers with competing offers for Merci. Marriage in India seemed to be first of all a business affair involving contracts and dowries. Love, if it came at all, came later.

Judy and I got another view of this marriage proposal business a few days later. We had an afternoon tea with Sangeetha, one of Augustine's newest, brightest, and most charming staff members. Judy and I both felt that Sangeetha could have a great future with Habitat for Humanity. Thinking along those lines and about the possibility of Sangeetha working one day at the headquarters in Americus, Judy asked Sangeetha if she had a passport. "Oh, Judy," Sangeetha said. Then she reached into her handbag, retrieved her billfold, and pulled out a folded newspaper clipping. Sangeetha then passed the clipping to Judy and told us that her father had contracted her marriage to an Indian citizen living in France, and she had gotten a passport to join him there once the wedding took place. But the clipping was a recent notice that the young man had taken out in the local paper, canceling the marriage contract. The young man had stated clearly that his change of mind had nothing to do with Sangeetha or her family. But in Sangeetha's tone of voice and in the downward cast of her eyes as she spoke, there was a story of damaged goods. "Judy, I do not know if I will ever marry." My heart sank. Here was one of the most beautiful and articulate young women I had met anywhere, and her future hung like a dark cloud over her head. Sangeetha's sadness in that moment reminded me of a sadness I had detected in Edwin, another of Augustine's employees, on the morning he reported that his wife had given birth to a daughter. India's race to a modern democratic society seemed greatly constrained by traditions of caste and marriage that would not let go.

After the dinner at Augustine's, Judy and I spent the night a nearby hotel. Driving back to Bangalore the next morning, I observed that Augustine seemed to be related closely to my father-in-law, in that he told the driver every turn and move to make. Turn here. Slow down. Pass now. Turn left. I am sure the driver who made this trip every day did not need directions for every move. I had seen signs that Augustine interacted with his staff in the same way he directed the driver. He had a strong tendency to micro-manage everything. This trait had served Augustine and Habitat India well during the first few years. It was Augustine's attention to detail and the unselfish gift of his time that had built the national board and staff since 1995. It was Augustine who opened the office and provided detailed handbooks and guides for employees and homeowner processes. But now it was Augustine's attention to detail that was holding back his staff and national partners, not giving them the latitude and responsibility and authority needed to propel Habitat India to the next level. I had learned the hard way many times in my business career that you are more likely to achieve success by hiring a person with the behavioral tendencies a job requires than by attempting to change someone programmed to go in a different direction. I doubted Augustine could change from a micro-manager to a macro-manager or leader and that Habitat India could grow successfully without such a change.

We ran behind schedule that day, but not because of Augustine's constant directions to his driver. It was just a typical traffic day in a country of one billion people. We had two important assignments. One was to attend a house dedication near Bangalore, and the other was to catch the 1:30 p.m. train to Mysore for a two-day retreat with the entire national staff. I was looking forward to the house dedication because it was going to be the first Habitat house Judy and I had seen in India. We arrived forty-five minutes late, but since Judy, Augustine, and I were participating in the dedication, everyone waited. As we got out of the car, Augustine asked Judy if she would present a Bible to the family. Bible presentations are customary at almost all Habitat dedications worldwide, but not so customary in a country where Christians had been killed recently for trying to convert Muslims and Hindus. Judy agreed to present the Bible. I had no idea what she was thinking, but it couldn't have been much, because five minutes later the ceremony was under way and it was Judy's turn to make her presentation.

It was obvious from the dress and tilaks that we were standing before a Hindu couple—in fact, a very distinguished-looking older couple. I was proud of my wife. As she presented the Bible to the stately man, she said, "Sir, this book tells the story that Habitat follows. It tells why we do what we do. It contains the wisdom and traditions of our faith. We know you have a different tradition but wanted to share ours with you." I wanted to congratulate Judy but assumed what she had said made little difference to homeowners who did not speak English. A puff of wind would have blown us over when the gentleman responded in perfect English, "Thank you, madam. We will take this book and read it and share it with our neighbors." Judy had scored a perfect ten with no chance to practice, and she had hit exactly the right tone for a Bible presentation in India.

With the ceremonies over, we were invited to tour the house, and the new homeowners offered refreshments, including Pepsi Cola, crackers, and slices of fruit. Our Habitat hosts took great care of us on this trip. At dedications and other times, if our hosts deemed the offered food to be unsafe for Judy and me, they would say, "No, thank you," for us, or indicate what we could safely try. As a result, we spent thirty days in India and never had any stomach distress.

The house was neat and clean; it was 240 square feet, including a kitchen, and combination sitting room and bedroom. A more complete and interesting description of an Indian Habitat house and its building process has been given in a letter of agreement between an affiliate and a homeowner provided by the Hyderabad affiliate:

1. The house will be 240 SFT (10X10, 10X8, 10X6). The foundation of the house will be constructed using rubble and cement.
2. The steps will be constructed using rubble and cement, and will be pointed with cement.
3. The walls of the house will be nine inches thick and ten feet high, and will be constructed using bricks/country burnt bricks to a thickness of five inches.
4. The house will be fitted with two walls almirahs [interior partitions] of brick/cement construction and will have three shelves. [These are interior partitions with built-in shelves two feet from the ceiling.]
5. The house will have three windows of two partitions each, with a height of four feet, and width of three feet, and windows will have ten milled steel bars horizontally fixed. There will be ventilation in the kitchen of 3.5' by 1.5'.
6. The house will have a cement roof of three inches thickness.
7. The walls within the rooms and interior will be plastered and the floors will be with shabad [stones] and plastered. The front of the house will also be plastered.

8. No decorations or red oxide will be permitted on the floor.

9. The kitchen slab will be six by three feet and will be fitted with two ovens, one of them being a smokeless oven.

10. There will be one latrine with bath room in the house compound and the side will be four and six feet with an Indian model closet. The latrine will be connected to a double leach pit, with alternative exit facilities.

11. There will be two doors to the house, fitted with ordinary latch and lock, and there will be no doors to the windows, which can be fitted by the buyer later.

12. The buyer needs to mobilize on his own the necessary rubble and timber for the house and to provide the necessary unskilled labor.

13. The buyer hereby agrees that no additions, or extra works to the house will be done, exceeding Rs. 1555/- in total for such extras, and hereby agrees to limit such extras to the works specified.

14. If the construction of the house gets suspended due to the non-cooperation of the buyer, Habitat, the project holder, shall not in any way be responsible for such breakdowns.

15. The buyer hereby agrees to transport the necessary materials which need to be taken from the warehouse to the site.

16. The buyer agrees to repay the full cost of the house in monthly installments of Rs. 320/- [during our trip U.S. $1 was worth Rs. 40] and agrees to pay a fine of 10% of all arrears at the end of any quarter.

17. The buyer agrees to contribute physical labor of not less than forty hours for the building of other Habitat houses in the locality, and thus to participate in the sweat equity of the project.

There were a few other clauses in this typical agreement. One focused on the fact that the buyer provided the land upon which the house was built, and another prevented the buyer from renting the house to a third party until it was paid for. I was impressed with the detail in the contract, the specifications, and the clarity of the buyer's responsibility. The existence of such a document was a strong testament to the literacy of the Indian people and the country's system of law. In a further effort to win the trust of the buyer and to demonstrate complete transparency, some Habitat affiliates took the additional step of permitting the home buyer and the construction supervisor to purchase the house materials together.

That first house we saw was typical of the more than fifty Habitat houses we visited while in India. A few had gable roofs as opposed to cement slabs. The gable roofs were less expensive but also less reliable in the monsoon seasons. But everywhere we heard that the Habitat houses were costing Rs. 15,000 to 20,000 more than the mortgage Habitat provided. This meant in many cases potential homeowners had to raise the additional funds from family or from moneylenders who charged exorbitant rates of interest, defeating the very purpose of Habitat's no-interest, no-profit approach to house building. In fact, while I attended the national board meeting in Hyderabad, thankfully, the board agreed to raise Habitat mortgages from Rs. 40,000 to 55,000.

I have probably told you more about a Habitat house in India than you want to know. But you should know that every house we saw had electricity and was near a source of potable water. This was not true for the Habitat houses in Ghana. The Indian government made land available to its citizens, and many new Habitat houses were built alongside the thatched houses where the families formerly lived and which were now occupied by the farm animals, for which they were fit. There was no greater testimony to the work of Habitat in India than to see this contrast of the before and after and to realize what a difference a simple, decent house of cement and stone can make to a family that once lived in a hut.

We traveled from Bangalore to Mysore by train. We were headed for the Pragatai Training Centre, a facility owned and operated by the Catholic Church for the organization and development of people. Judy and I were accompanied by Augustine and Josephine and members of Augustine's Bangalore staff. The national partners had to find their way to Mysore by bus. On the train we sat in reserved cars and enjoyed spacious seats. But most of the cars were jammed with people hanging out the windows and doors. Augustine paid particular attention to the travel plans and safety of the women, for he knew that their fathers and families would hold him accountable if anything happened to them on this trip. The men were not so fortunate. Our train ride took three hours. The national partners who came by bus from other Indian cities endured an eighteen-hour ride to Mysore and at the end of our two-day meeting would spend another eighteen hours getting home. The difficulty, cost, and time associated with travel made me wonder how anyone in Augustine's role could ever mentor or direct his staff. How could he even be in their presence enough to influence their work? I had always taken pride in talking with my managers face-to-face, listening, sharing, and working side by side. India obviously required a totally different approach.

As the train rumbled through the countryside, we saw a different part of India. We were in a farming area where grain and rice grew. In South India it is possible to produce three rice crops a year. In fact, while we were there, this country of one billion people was a net exporter of food rice and other foodstuffs.

We reached Mysore in the late afternoon and registered at the retreat center. Mysore has a population approaching three-quarters of a million and is known for its silk and sandalwood. At one time, Mysore was the seat of the maharajas of Mysore, who had constructed a walled Indo-Saracenic palace. The evening program included a devotional song; a Bible reading; a message by John Bell, an international partners and a former Presbyterian minister; the lighting of the lamp; a welcome and introductory message by Augustine; self-introductions by all participants; the sharing of responsibilities and the formation of a steering committee for the retreat; greetings from Judy and me; and a concluding prayer. The retreat had a double focus. First, we were going to examine the qualities of a good leader as exemplified in Jesus and then by modern writers. Second, we were going to examine the Habitat program in India to see what was broken and how it could be fixed. To get started the next morning, we also would review the resolutions the group had made at the previous retreat.

Here is what I learned: In India, you do not challenge the word of your national director. When he enters the room, you stand up. When he tells you to "come out" and tell him what you think, you remain silent. When he points and raves about improvements that are needed and reports that have not been made, you look down. After an hour or two of this the first morning, I spoke privately with Augustine and suggested that we break into groups and ask the groups to discuss the issues and then report back after we reassembled. This is a strategy that had worked for me in my Crosland days, when Mr. Crosland's leadership style had shut off debate. And it worked in India. When group members were freed from the need to confront the director head-on, suggestions, criticisms, and energy flowed from everyone, and the group recorders were able to report back their findings in a non-threatening way. I later talked to Augustine about using this breakout method to improve his chance of getting honest feedback, but the concept was too foreign.

The groups reported many frustrations. The affiliates were not re-sponding to the national office with timely reports, proposals, or news stories. The national partners, who worked for Augustine throughout India and who were to be overseeing affiliate development and commit-tees, appeared powerless. The affiliate committees would not listen to them, and they seemed to have a lot more responsibility than authority. Many of the affiliate committees had a member who served on the national Habitat board, and that member often seemed to use the national partner to do family selection or perform some other function for his affiliate, as opposed to expanding Habitat to other communities. Augustine wanted to know why the cost of houses was increasing and what was being done about it. He was upset to hear that homeowners were borrowing half the cost of their houses from others. It became clear that Habitat India was going nowhere fast until the role and the responsibility of the national partners were defined and accepted at all levels, starting with the national board and Augustine and including each affiliate and the staff in Augustine's office. But given the dynamics of Augustine's management style and the board members' practice of using the national partners to serve the ends of their own affiliates, I could not discern a path through this thicket. Already Augustine was talking about adding zone managers to oversee the national partners, and I was asking myself, "To what end?"

Outside the retreat sessions Judy and I had the chance to get to know some of the staff members on a deeper level. We also enjoyed a visit to Brindavan Gardens, which stretch out below the Krishnaraja Sagar dam with many illuminated fountains. Other side trips took us to the Mysore Palace, with its intricate wood carvings and gilded mirrors. The current palace was completed in 1912 to replace an earlier palace that burned in 1897. Thirty-one hundred feet above Mysore, Chamundi Hill and the Sri Chamundeswari Temple gave us expanded views not only of the surrounding landscape but also of the religious traditions of Mysore. These trips deepened our sense of the rich history and culture of this fascinating land.

On Sunday afternoon we returned by train to Bangalore, where we spent the night before flying to Hyderabad to attend the meeting of the Habitat India national board and to visit the Bonghir and Secunderbad affiliates. Hyderabad is the capital of Andhra Pradesh and is at the cen-ter of the Muslim culture and tradition in India. Here the literacy rate is only 45 percent, and much of the state is economically depressed. We were met at the Hyderabad airport by Rev. G. John and his wife,

Theeba. G. John chaired the India national board and was president of the Secunderbad Affiliate. He and Theeba were also the founders of COUNT (Christian Outreach to Native Tribes), a nonprofit organization based in Hyderabad that ran a boarding school for eight hundred tribal children. The school focused on literacy and trades as well as Bible instruction. Graduates from the school had planted more than 150 churches in the tribal forests of India. As I learned, in India the tribal people fall below the caste system and generally live in the forest in rural areas. They are below the untouchables, and here was a gentle man and his wife bringing dignity and love to people considered outcasts of society. I asked G. John why Hindus and others were so opposed to Christianity, and he said that it was because of the personal transformation Christian converts felt. G. John said that appearances and attitudes changed, and the new members of the Christian community were no longer subservient to the caste system. Judy and I both were moved by G. John, Theeba, and the school. We later gave financial support to COUNT and hosted G. John on a fund-raising trip to the United States. G. John and Theeba served as most gracious hosts, even taking us shopping and later buying us gifts they surely could not have afforded.

But the gentle John of COUNT was not so gentle when it came to Habitat's national board, which he ran with an iron fist. I use the term *board* loosely, because at the time of my visit, there were only five existing members of what had been a twelve-member board, and G. John was their spokesman. I did enjoy the day I spent with the board and appreciated the opportunity to speak to them about strategic planning and the future direction of Habitat for Humanity International. It was also a time for me to listen. I shared with the board four issues I asked them to consider:

1. As quickly as possible expand from five to twelve members, adding more diversity and experience by reaching out to the business community rather than to presidents of affiliate committees.
2. Take the new and expanded board through a visioning and planning process so that all would share a common vision and plan for Habitat India.
3. Define the roles of the national partners and specify their responsibilities and authority as well as reporting relationships.
4. Provide leadership in reaching out to businesses and the total community by telling Habitat's story and soliciting support. (In my thinking, this was the only way for the program to grow.)

The board took note of my thoughts and then presented some stronger requests of their own for me to deliver to the international board:

1. Will Habitat International look at its allocation of funds based on need for housing rather than on a country-by-country basis? (India contains one-sixth of the world's population. Three hundred fifty million people live in thatched huts or tents. The physical size of the country dwarfed many other nations. A regional zone in India would be larger than many other countries and require the same administrative support. I had asked them to raise more funds internally, and they had told me the need was so great that no matter what they did, Habitat International had to do more.)

2. Will Habitat's international board and staff provide India with its impressions of Habitat India's performance, recognizing strengths as well as weaknesses? (In other words, we have heard enough about our shortcomings; what are we are doing right?)

3. Will Habitat International provide opportunities for interchange visits among national boards, staffs, and affiliate committees on a worldwide basis? We want to see how others are making Habitat work.

4. Will Habitat International entrust Habitat India with responsibility as a partner and grant Habitat India freedom to respond to local situations and challenges, especially in relation to house guidelines?

5. Will Habitat International provide special project funding for block-making machines and equipment for fly ash brick?

6. Will Habitat International make an effort to gain and demonstrate a greater understanding of the issues faced by India? An example of this lack of understanding took place at this board meeting. Todd Garth, Habitat's regional director of South Asia, informed the India board that the following week the U.S. Congress was likely to appropriate $1.6 million to house Tibetan refugees in India. Little information was available, but the India board was asked to indicate its willingness to accept funds for this project and to respond within a matter of days. The India board was mindful of the pressure on Habitat International to accept such funds, but this board had some significant questions of its own. What might the government of India think, and how might it react? What will Indians living in the area think if we assist the Tibetans and not the

Indians? And there were a host of other questions for which there was no time or opportunity to develop answers.

7. Will Habitat International involve Habitat India in the selection and approval of international partners assigned to India?

This board had more questions for me than I had for them, and each of their questions merited serious consideration. Underlying all of the questions seemed to be a sense of frustration and even anger at unequal treatment as a partner in the work of Habitat and the lack of freedom to develop local guidelines. I have to acknowledge that my report to Steve Weir and Habitat's international board and staff changed nothing of significance and that my suggestions to the India board produced about the same results there. The unfortunate upshot of all this is that as of this moment, six years later, Habitat International has gone through the painful and regretful process of disaffiliating itself from the program it started in India and is working with some local affiliate committees to restart and grow the program. In the midst of all the charges and countercharges that have been exchanged are ones involving the misuse of funds that reach into the top ranks of Habitat India. Everyone is wondering how we got to this point. I think I know. We failed to develop a true partnership with the India national board. While the issues between Habitat International and Habitat India's former board members wind through the legal system, Habitat International has set up a new organization in India and is building at an accelerated pace.

The tone, the feel, the vision, the challenge facing affiliate committees in India was captured for me in this brief welcoming speech from the president of the Nalgonda Habitat for Humanity, Bhongir, when we visited with the committee on the morning of June 30, 1999.

In the name of our Lord Saviour Jesus Christ, I the president, the committee members, and the staff of NHFH, Bhongir, welcome Mrs. Mr. Paul Leonard, treasurer, International HFH; Rev. G. John, chairman, HFH India; and the executive director, Mr. P. Augustine, HFH India, to our affiliate NHFH, Bhongir. It gives me immense pleasure to invite you to the Bhongir affiliate. We feel happy to have you with us this morning. We are very thankful to you for sparing your precious time to visit our affiliate and get to know each other and the work going on in Bhongir.

I would like to give you a brief note about the NHFH, Bhongir. Bhongir is a town with a population of one lakh [100,000], mainly daily bread earners and low-income groups, such as factory labourers, etc. Providing shelter and demonstrating the love and teaching of our Lord Jesus Christ is the primary object and concern of NHFH, Bhongir, to all homeless and needy families, regardless of caste, creed, and religion.

The Habitat Mission, which was started in the year 1992, built 48 houses, and there was a gap of three years and again the work revived in the year 1997. Since then we have built 33 houses which are occupied and 33 houses which are under construction. At present 35 applications are under process to reach a target of 150 houses by the end of 1999. Of them 78 are Hindus, 24 are Christian, and 12 are Muslims and a total of 114 houses. We provide a low-cost house with an area of 260 square feet, that has two rooms and kitchen with bathroom and latrine costing Rs. 40,000/- from the affiliate loan, payable with a period of six and half years. The repayments are used to build more houses for the needy.

Now we are planning partnership with other non-governmental organisations to become self-sustainable and eliminate the poverty of housing in the District of Nalgonda.

The local churches (i.e., Christian Gospel Church, Manna Church, the Hebron Church, and St. Thomas C.S.I. Churches) are supporting the Habitat ministry through prayer in their respective churches regularly. The committee is also making a planned program for the resource development from various churches, organisations, and business establishments within Bhongir to construct one house per year.

We wish and pray that this noble task which the Lord has started here in Bhongir will continue for the glory and honour of our Lord and Saviour Jesus Christ to fulfill the vision of our founder, President Mr. Millard Fuller, and the HFH International. So far the Lord has really helped us to overcome many obstacles and press forward to fill this great mission.

I take this opportunity to thank all the honorable guests from abroad and India for being with us and making this a memorable occasion for NHFH, Bhongir. Thank you one and all.

From every affiliate committee we visited, we heard a similar speech, warm in its welcome, passionate about the Lord and his work, humble in its spirit and focused in its vision. The speeches, the handshakes, and the smiles on the people's faces deepened my sense of awe about the world and its people, as well as about Habitat's ability to reach into hearts and minds on every continent. Just rereading this speech and writing about this experience takes me back to the sights and sounds of these Indian villages and people. I can see myself standing next to a new Habitat family and a house beside a well at the end of a footpath one hundred yards from the road, basking in the joy and hope that a simple, decent house brings to faraway places.

July is not the most desirable season to travel in the south of India—unless you are into daily saunas and enjoy high humidity and temperatures exceeding one hundred degrees. It was on one of those days before we left Hyderabad that G. John and Augustine took Judy and me to the Dhomaiguda community fifteen kilometers from Hyderabad. We went there for a groundbreaking, and I have a great picture of Judy in a salwar kameez, the casual dress of an Indian woman, jabbing an iron pole into the ground to start work on a new house. But the most beautiful sight that day was that of Hindu, Muslim, and Christian families living side by side in peace in their Habitat homes. Dhomaiguda demonstrated even more than Belfast the reconciling power of Habitat. For me, Dhomaiguda remains both a symbol of what Habitat India has accomplished and, even more important, a sign of the future our world must build if it is to survive.

A Model Affiliate

On July 5, 1999, Judy and I flew to Chennai (Madras) to visit a Habitat community and to sightsee. We left Augustine at Hyderabad and were met in Chennai by Anna Charley, one of the national partners. This was our first chance since being in India to travel with other staff members and begin to understand Habitat India through the eyes of those who were trying to nurture and grow the affiliates. Charley was over six feet tall with broad shoulders, dark skin, and a great laugh. Charley loved life. He had been the joker at the retreat in Mysore, and it was fun to travel with him. So Judy and I did what Charley wanted to do. For a day he took our minds off Habitat. We went for a boat ride. We visited a reptile farm and saw crocodiles and a cobra handler. We rode the rides at the Dizzy World Amusement Park. We acted like kids. We visited one of the most astounding, mystical, and moving shrines in all of India, the shore temple at Mahabalipuram, an ancient capital seaport of the first significant Tamil Dynasty. Here beside the sea, carved out of stone during the seventh and eighth centuries, were scenes from everyday life, a life-size tiger and elephant, and several temples and shrines. Stone carving was still prevalent in the area, and shops abounded where intricate rock carvings could be seen and purchased.

We spent that night in Chennai. Augustine flew in the next morning, and after we met him at the airport, Charley took us to see the houses and families of Chennai Habitat. Several homes were under construction, and others had been finished recently. We could see the joy of these families in their faces, and we received their warm and loving greetings. Not far from the community, rice was growing in flooded green fields shaded by palm trees. After a quick trip to the airport, we flew with Augustine to Trichy.

If Habitat India has a true success story, it is Trichy Habitat. Formed in 1997, in two years this affiliate, led by a former Catholic priest, had completed 165 homes. Before attending an evening dedication of twenty houses, which included a Hindu wedding ceremony, Judy and I met with the affiliate committee. Every committee member had made a financial contribution to Habitat, and six of the members had paid their own way to the Jimmy Carter Work Project held earlier that year in the Philippines. One of their subcommittees had persuaded a local cement company to lower the price on its bags of cement from 185 to 130 rupees per bag. The affiliate was also working with a government program to get funding for the construction of latrines. They had another partnership that supplied a cow or buffalo for each Habitat family to assist the family in their income generation and to provide further security for house repayments. I had never seen a more highly energized or motivated group, or seen a Habitat affiliate focusing on community and families as much as it was on house building.

Upon arrival, we visited a rural Habitat community and saw many of the grass huts that the Habitat families previously occupied. One touching moment during our visit occurred when we approached a new house and the priest asked that we stop and pray for the homeowner. Her husband had recently been electrocuted by an irrigation pump. When the woman saw us, she began to cry, and I reached out and embraced her. Then she moved to Judy and, sobbing, threw her arms around Judy's neck. Later Augustine said that he could not have embraced the woman as I did, but the fact that I did it had made a favorable impression on the community. Grief and sorrow have no boundaries.

The spirit present in that day's meeting and community visit carried over into the next evening's celebration with a band, singing, and the dedication of twenty new Habitat homes. Two hundred people had gathered before an elevated stage where Judy and I sat with other speakers, guests of honor, and a very frightened young Hindu man and woman dressed in bright red and gold and sitting near us on throne-like chairs. We soon discovered that we would be participating not only in ribbon cuttings and house dedications but also in the marriage ceremony of this young man and woman, who were the owners of one of the new homes. The speaker announced that both the dedication and the wedding were timed to occur after 6:00 p.m., because after that hour the stars and moon would be aligned and it would be the auspicious or proper time for the wedding. As the wedding progressed, Judy and I were asked to stand before the couple and tie a string binding their hands together. And it must have been an auspicious time, because we got the job done even though I have never seen two more frightened young people in my life. Judy presented the bride with one of the ten shawls she had received as gifts during our travels, and I gave the groom a twenty-dollar bill. These gestures on our part began to dissolve some of the tension in those young faces, but I was reminded again that we were witnessing a marriage born out of a parental contract and not necessarily love's desire.

We left Trichy in the company of Augustine and a driver headed for a seminary in Madurai, where we were to join John Bell, a Habitat international partner who developed new affiliate committees. After stopping three times for directions and traveling in circles for thirty minutes, we found John and the seminary. Habitat distinguishes between an international and a national partner. A national partner, such as Anna Charley, was a native of the country in which he worked and was compensated at local wage rates. Most international partners, such as John Bell, were from the United States or other Western countries. Some worked as volunteers receiving modest stipends for housing, food, and travel, and others worked as full-time employees compensated at western pay rates. This system had led to great inequality in pay for people who had identical work assignments, which was the case with Charley and John. It also had led to differential treatment by the Habitat India board members and affiliate committees, and it made genuine cooperation and respect among the national and international partners more difficult. Since the Asia-Pacific office was directed and run mostly by Westerners, it paid more attention to the concerns and suggestions of international partners. The roots of this staffing scheme stemmed from Habitat's earliest days, when international partners had provided the only way for Habitat to launch programs overseas. As Habitat grew, national partners were added, but it had become obvious that a more equitable staffing system was required.

At the seminary we attended an organizing meeting for a new affiliate committee. Augustine explained Habitat's principles and concepts, and both Augustine and John answered questions. Ten to twelve people attended, including a few local teachers and preachers. It was obvious from the questions and answers that a lot more work would be required before this group could select its first family and build its first house. But everyone left with an assignment, and a time was set for the next meeting. We said good-bye to Augustine, hopped into John's car, and headed for the Hosanna Children's Home, a boarding school and orphanage run by John's friend the Reverend Emmanuel. A hundred smiling faces greeted us that afternoon as we toured the grounds and vegetable garden. The children's noisy energy bounced off the compound's walls as they ran and screamed during recess. But it took only a few commands from the reverend and a teacher to restore order. We attended evening vespers, ate with the children, and slept in the reverend's bed. We learned that most of the children came from Christian families in the state of Tamil Nadu that were experiencing some form of persecution and saw the school as a safe haven for their children. Much of the financial support for the school had come from the United States and especially from a church in Florence, South Carolina, led by one of Emmanuel's seminary classmates. This home did not appear to be run with the same degree of order, purpose, and vision as G. John's boarding school in Hyderabad. We were shown a site for a future infirmary and indirectly encouraged to support the fund-raising efforts. Neither Judy nor I was convinced.

But the next morning, before we left for the Kovalam affiliate on India's south coast, John and the Reverend Emmanuel took us to a small community at the foot of a mountain forest and there introduced us to some of India's forest people, the type of families COUNT was serving. It was a clear, bright morning, early enough for us to still appreciate the night's cooling effect. John had explained that these families had lived not long ago in the mountain forest and had sustained themselves by clearing the forest and selling its wood. The Indian government had a program to discourage this harvesting of forest and had relocated the families to the foot of the mountain and provided fields for them to grow crops. John and Emmanuel hoped that Habitat might start building in this village and help these families replace their hovels. A community well dug by the government had collapsed, and the families had to walk more than a mile to draw their water from a polluted stream. I could see no sources of income for these families, and therefore no hope that Habitat could build here and expect its mortgage loans to be repaid. John and Emmanuel were clearly disappointed by this news, and I was distressed by the plight of these people. It has been a source of some small consolation to me that upon my return to Mooresville, I worked with my local Rotary and a Rotary in India to provide a bore well and pump for the people of this village.

After we left this village, Judy and I were approaching the end of our visits to local Habitat affiliates. We spent two more nights with John, one on the Periyar Tiger Preserve located on a British hill station and another at India's southern tip, where we saw a stunning sunset over the Indian Ocean. The cities and villages we passed through teemed with life. Tailors, mechanics, and shopkeepers worked late into the night. Signs everywhere carried the pictures of army and air force service personnel killed in the ongoing war with Pakistan and announced the times and places of their funerals. These signs and the daily news associated with the war gave us a new appreciation for Indian nationalism and pride and laid down a marker for our own sense of nationalism and pride that grew out of the events of September 11, 2001, in our country.

When Judy and I left Delhi, Jacqueline Lundquist had promised to arrange a relaxing trip to Jaipur and Agra. Upon our return to Delhi, a driver, car, and reservations were in order for an unbelievable ending to what had already been an extraordinary adventure.

I will leave it to the experienced architects and historians to describe the majesty, beauty and importance of the Taj Mahal and the fort at Agra. I can simply say that I could have sat on the ground and looked at the Taj Mahal for the rest of my life and been at peace. I have never seen a more perfectly proportioned or more beautifully decorated building or more magical reflecting pools. We discovered on this last trip how ambassadors travel. Jacqueline's choice for a hotel exceeded any imaginable standard for luxury: an attendant dedicated to each guest, a bath opened to a walled flower garden, swimming pools stunning in their beauty, and grounds immaculately decorated with every color and fragrance of flower. It was difficult to make sense out of the wealth that created these places and the poverty we had experienced in every city, town, and village that marked our path through India. Yet I know that the extremes of wealth and poverty we saw here crisscross this world in ways that must mystify the One who created us as equals. We saw more tents, more shacks, more people sleeping in doorways and on sidewalks, more beggars, more slums, more open sewers, more pollution, more traffic than we had seen in any other country. We also saw more food, more energy, more vitality, more diversity, more excitement, more hospitality, more trade, and more wealth than we had seen in any other country. India encompassed both poverty and wealth, and Habitat India would have to focus on both to become a truly vital force in that country.

On July 18, exactly thirty days after we had first arrived in India, Judy and I were airborne for home.

Fifteen months later we returned to Hyderabad for the fall meeting of Habitat's international board. Our stay this time was all business and no sightseeing. But the return to Hyderabad was preceded by another A-Team build in Pokara, Nepal. We had changed planes in Delhi on the way to Katmandu. Thankfully, our earlier experience in India had equipped me for the struggle with Air India and a bungled plane reservation. After a threat to use another airline, our tickets were approved and we met our group at the Astoria Hotel in Katmandu. The next day we flew on Buddha Air, skirting the Himalayas on the way north to Pokara. The views of the mountain range and the fields below were magnificent.

Our work in Nepal centered on two houses, one at the foundation stage and the other nearing completion. The Pokara affiliate was led by Major (Retired) Keshav Tamang, who had served many years in the British Army, and he ran the affiliate as a major would, with order and dignity. Buddhiman, a local volunteer, handled all the arrangements for and directed our work camp. At each gathering Buddhiman would provide a warm greeting and then introduce the next steps by saying, "And so, distinguished guests, let's get on the bus," or "And so, let's mix the cement. . . ." We all fell in love with this kind and funny man who on one occasion wore two billed caps, with the bills pointed left and right. Buddhiman had served as a personal assistant to a colonel in the British Army. The colonel had retired in Pokara and literally adopted Buddhiman as his son. Buddhiman was now a wealthy man, but his good fortune had not changed his loving and gentle nature.

The Habitat houses in Nepal were very similar to those in India, but the rocky soil made excavations extremely difficult. The rural setting of Pokara, with the mountains as an eastern backdrop, helped us understand why trekkers love this country. A Hindu served on the local affiliate board, and in some small way Habitat was learning how to reach beyond the religious walls that divided this community. But the Hindu-led government in Nepal did not permit the presentation of Bibles to

Habitat homeowners. Habitat has had to learn to adapt its approach to local customs in many places, and it is this ability to adapt that keeps it growing. It will be difficult to forget the beautiful children who came each day to the work sites to watch us work and to play or the Nepalese families who worked beside us.

I would trade the heat of Hyderabad for the cool of Pokara any day.

PART 3

A LARGER VISION

20

AMERICUS: HABITAT CENTRAL

When Judy and I went to Kenya on a photo safari, the drive from Nairobi to Amboseli was particularly challenging. Paved roads gave way to unpaved roads and unpaved roads to tracks where previous travelers turned and made their own road. My directions for getting to Amboseli are, "Go to the end of the earth and turn right." If you cannot find Amboseli, you can go to the other end of the earth, turn left, and arrive in Americus, Georgia, the headquarters of Habitat for Humanity International. Americus is located in the southwestern section of the state about three hours from Atlanta. Millard often said that finding one's way to Americus is a good test of commitment, and we know that anyone who arrives there is serious.

I have had several introductions to Americus. The first was during a major donor weekend in the spring of 1995. I represented Centex at an annual appreciation event held in Americus. The highlights of the weekend were dinner and an evening with President and Mrs. Carter, including photographs, and a Sunday morning visit to President Carter's Sunday school class at the Maranatha Baptist Church. A tour of Habitat's Americus facilities included the Rylander Building, the Clarence Jordan Center, numerous volunteer houses, and the International Village.

During my first visit I was most impressed with the International Village, which included models of Habitat houses built in Latin America, India, and Africa. We saw a brick press used in Africa to make mud bricks and listened to docents describe daily life in the various countries. These model homes contained three to four hundred square feet divided into two to four rooms and made a significant impression on me. In other words, each house was only 25 percent to 30 percent of the size of Habitat homes in the United States. The toilet facilities consisted of a latrine/outhouse. Except for the Indian house, cooking also took place outside the home. Signs in this village demonstrated Habitat's concept of appropriate technology—that is, using materials and building techniques common to each country as a way of containing costs and making the self-help building strategy work around the world. Here in less than an acre, I glimpsed Habitat's international work and gained a deeper appreciation for the scope and complexity of its mission.

A few years later, after my retirement from Centex, I had the opportunity to accompany Jonathan Wheeler and Neil Devroy, two new Centex executives, to Americus. The purpose of the trip was to orient Jon and Neil, who had no previous knowledge of Centex's partnership with Habitat for Humanity. For Centex to continue its support, it was critical to impress Jon and Neil with Habitat's purpose and scope. The one place I wanted them to see was the International Village, which, as I hoped, turned their heads. After they heard David Haskell, former director of Habitat Middle East, describe his work in Lebanon and Jordan and his motivation, Habitat had their attention. Jon turned to me as David concluded his talk at the morning's devotion and asked, "To whom do I write the check?"

Today Habitat has an even more impressive version of its International Village. We call it the Global Village and Discovery Center, and it is located next to the Clarence Jordan Center and a new railroad station built by the City of Americus to accompany a new short-line tourist train that runs from Interstate I-75 to Jimmy Carter's birthplace near Plains. Millard spoke eloquently about the potential of this new and expanded International Village because it included not only more examples of Habitat houses built around the globe (up to thirty-five upon completion) but also a slum village that dramatically shows the plight of 1.3 billion people in this world.

When the national media got word of what they called a "slum theme park," a few right-wing radio commentators took aim at Habitat and ridiculed the project. Their comments brought unprecedented publicity to this Americus location, most of which has been extremely favorable, but it is difficult to predict the long-term benefit to be gained from this costly expansion of the International Village. Cost overruns in the project's first phase were significant and violated a number of board resolutions regarding project fund-raising goals and borrowing limits. The original business plan for the Global Village and Discovery Center projected fifty to sixty thousand visitors per year. During the last three years of operation annual attendance ranged from fifteen to eighteen thousand. The truth is that the Global Village and Discovery Center is a great facility offering a moving experience to those who find it. Its problem is that we built it in the wrong location. Atlanta or Orlando would have been infinitely better choices. In the spring of 2005 upon the staff's recommendation, Habitat's board approved a scaled-back operating plan that would keep the Global Village open for self-guided tours while no longer promoting it as a tourist destination.

I made another trip to Americus for my second international board meeting in the summer of 1996. The main focus of this meeting was financial: approving the budget and setting policy that required monthly reports and defined variances that staff was required to report to the finance committee. Funds were tight, and part of the contingency plan approved in Manila was already in effect. The budget encompassed several priorities. Some involved strengthening the financial position, including a broader revenue base, a stable cash flow, the funding of an operating reserve, and the elimination of debt. Others aimed at strengthening the organization's structure, filling key vacancies, providing training, improving financial controls, and developing a worldwide vision in concert with the new awareness of and emphasis on global Habitat.

The board chair also made good on his promise to improve Habitat's focus on the world by reorganizing our board committees and creating a Global Policy Committee with six geographically focused subcommittees. Chairs of each of the area subcommittees would form the Global Policy Committee, which would resolve issues of alignment and common policies.

At this board meeting, I got to know more of the staff in both formal and informal sessions. I began to hear through these conversations and through the report of the Human Resource Committee how difficult it was to recruit new employees to Americus. Not many highly sought prospective employees or their families welcomed the charm of a small

Southern town or county, especially when its school system ranked at the bottom in a state ranked in almost the same place. I have looked for the pluses of living in Americus but find few beyond the history that surrounds Koinonia Farms, Habitat's birthplace, and nearby Plains, Jimmy Carter's birthplace. Americus had a long history of opposition to civil rights, some of it violent. In fact, Americus has shown little appreciation for Habitat until recently. Millard traveled and spoken widely around the world, but only in the past few years was he invited to speak at a church in Americus. My suspicion is that Habitat has become such a significant economic force in the city and county that the leaders are now paying more attention. Habitat has to be one of the largest employers in the county and is likely the largest landowner in the city.

Beginning in 1998, Habitat decentralized its international operations, setting up regional offices in San Jose, Pretoria, Budapest, and Bangkok. These moves resolved the Americus problem for the families that left, but a serious problem exists for those who remain, and for the future of an international organization whose success will depend on the quality and capability of the people it can employ.

I have a deep appreciation for the history and roots that Americus represents, not only for the vision, work, and sacrifices of Millard and Linda, but also for many of the Habitat families and employees who reside there. In many ways Americus and Sumter County have provided a laboratory where projects like the Sumter County Initiative, a partnership to virtually eliminate substandard housing in the county, were created and were successful. Habitat will always need such testing grounds, but they do not all have to be in Americus. Americus can serve many of our back office and operational needs and provide a good location for Habitat University, a new program with emphasis on leadership education that offers courses over the Internet. But Habitat requires competent managers to develop and operate its information system, financial, communications, and resource development departments and ultimately will have to find a home closer to Atlanta or another major city to attract such talent. Not surprisingly, for Millard such thoughts bordered on heresy. It is one of the differences we had about Habitat's future. Out of deference to the founder, the board chose not to press the headquarters location issue, but less than nine months after Millard's termination, the board voted to move the administrative headquarters to Atlanta and leave its operational headquarters in Americus. While Jonathan Reckford, our new CEO, will have an office in both locations, he and his family will live in Atlanta.

21

CHICAGO

Judy and I left Chicago in June 1964, headed for Charlotte, North Carolina, in our 1957 black Volkswagen Beatle. Never has a little car carried such a big load. Amy was two months old and either sat in Judy's lap or slept on half of the backseat. The other half of the backseat and the floor and area under the seat carried everything we could not put in the luggage carrier. Before we got into Indiana, sparks came from the battery compartment under the rear seat. We stopped and rearranged the load. Before we got to Indianapolis, the car overheated, and we stopped to discover that the ironing board I had wedged between the top of the car and the bottom of the luggage rack had prevented the ventilation necessary for the rear-mounted, air-cooled engine. The service station attendant became the proud owner of a used ironing board.

There were other delays and problems along the way to the point that Judy and I wondered if we would ever arrive in Charlotte, but we did. And we liked Charlotte so much that in forty-one years we never moved beyond its metropolitan area.

I had returned to Chicago once in the late 1960s to attend a conference at the Divinity School. The day before the conference, Chicago was hit by the snowstorm of the century. O'Hare was closed to air traffic, and thousands of stranded passengers spent the night at the airport. I flew in the next morning unaware of the storm's impact and the conference's cancellation. I realized the magnitude of the snowfall when I got off the elevated train on 55th Street and started walking to the Divinity School. Cars parked along the side streets were no longer visible except for the roofs. As I walked down the middle of these streets, the car tops did not come up to my knees. For a Florida boy, that is a lot of snow. Dean Brauer took me to dinner that night, and the next day I flew home.

My strongest memories of Chicago include the fight over a parking space we witnessed on our first trip to the Loop and the soot on the windowsill each winter morning. I also remember taking the car battery up to our apartment every night in the cold of winter and walking two miles in below-zero temperatures to deliver what I am sure was a frozen specimen to Judy's internist. The best part of Chicago was the trip to Madison to visit our Davidson friends, Perrin and Mary Jo Wright, who were in graduate school at the University of Wisconsin. The trip reminded us that trees, flowers, and fresh air still flourished, and it gave us hope that there might still be life outside of Chicago.

On October 17, 1996, Habitat for Humanity International brought me back to Chicago for its fall board meeting. I heard Millard deliver the first of several challenges he issued repeatedly to the board over the next eight years, focused on two points. He wanted us to know that income was rising and house numbers were flat. He also cautioned the board to continue to pay modest salaries to staff. Contrary to Millard's advice before the conclusion of the meeting, the board approved a proposal from the Human Resource Committee to raise the salary ranges 5 percent over the next three years and to create a new salary grade for its senior officers. More important, the board began to hear about an Urban Initiative to increase Habitat's effectiveness in cities like Chicago, Cleveland, Philadelphia, and Baltimore. Over time it became apparent that this announcement of an urban emphasis had more bark than bite, and more public relations than resources for action. We also received a high-level report on the direction of Project Impact, a pro bono assessment by McKinsey and Company of Habitat for Humanity's program and management. McKinsey was zeroing in on three issues: aligning common functions, dedicating a full set of resources to management issues, and decentralizing worldwide operations. The report noted the need for a mission statement for headquarters staff and a succession plan for Jimmy Carter and Millard Fuller. When McKinsey's report was completed and presented to the board some months later, its adoption radically altered Habitat's operations.

In Chicago, I got my first glimpse of some of the underlying tension between the board and the founder. It was over the Sumter County Initiative, Habitat's program to eliminate substandard housing in Sumter County, Georgia. In a difficult fund-raising period, there had been no restraining or reassessment of this initiative in spite of a slowdown in house-building transfers to our international affiliates. This concerned many on the board, but not Millard. Unkind words were spoken, feelings hurt. Then the board set a cap of $400,000 on the spending of undesignated funds for the Sumter County Initiative.

We elected new officers in Chicago, and after being on the board for less than a year, I was elected treasurer, which meant I would also chair the Finance Committee. The problems of overspending on Sumter County, underspending on employee salaries, and flat house-building numbers were headed my way. Chicago had fixed me one more time, and it had not yet finished with me.

Treasurers and finance committee chairs get a somewhat closer view of budgets and variances. One of the variances that began to occur in the spring of 1997 was the unplanned advance of $48,000 to Uptown Habitat, Chicago, which appeared in serious financial straits. Habitat for Humanity International got involved because Chicago is a major media market, and both United Airlines and Allstate had funded projects there that were both stalled and over budget. Millard and the board asked me to go have a look. I visited with the Uptown affiliate on June 12 and 13 and again on June 24 and 26. The Warren Boulevard project, which United Airlines had supported, required $600,000 for project completion, and the construction lender had stopped funding construction. The money provided by Allstate for the Kamerling III project had been spent, and construction had not started. Given the complexity of developing and building in an urban environment, the problems faced by our Uptown affiliate were not surprising. The affiliate was in over its head. The staff had grown in size, and fund-raising had fallen. Affiliate board members were burned out, and no easy answers appeared.

The strength of Habitat for Humanity is its challenge to local communities to launch Habitat affiliates and raise their own funds. This entrepreneurial approach has enabled Habitat to spread now to over 1,670 locations in the Unites States and another 900 locations elsewhere. That strength of Habitat for Humanity is also its weakness. Uptown Habitat did not have to listen to the advice of Habitat for Humanity's regional or national staff or its treasurer. Every recommendation became a matter of drawn-out negotiations, moves, and countermoves. Ultimately the projects were completed—Kamerling by another housing group—and Uptown Habitat merged with other Chicago affiliates.

My nine-page report to Millard and the board included detailed recommendations. One was to restructure the Warren Boulevard project, adding three more units and repricing the unsold units to recover more cost. I also believed reducing the number of affiliate staff was critical, as well as increasing the number of affiliate board members and bringing new life and enthusiasm onto the board. More important, I made several observations and recommendations about Habitat's work in the urban setting:

Many of the Habitat supporters I met expressed concerns that were much broader than Warren Boulevard or even the survival of Uptown. In fact, several thought that Uptown would not survive unless it changed the approach to the urban challenge. Habitat's efforts in Chicago, for example, have been harmed by the inability of the inner-city affiliates to cooperate with each other and the absence of any structure or system to coordinate city-wide activities.

Effective fund-raising in Chicago requires a unified approach. Affiliates working on their own can fund-raise for a house or two, but they are not effective in tapping corporate and foundation contributions. Prior attempts to fund-raise in Chicago on an umbrella basis have been defeated by lack of cooperation among area affiliates. Corporations and businesses are not likely to make significant contributions to Habitat without being challenged by a specific project in a specific location. Such a project needs to have a blitz quality to it and be of a size and importance that commands attention. How can Habitat in Chicago, Philadelphia, Newark, etc. structure itself to take advantage of this urban reality?

In Chicago blighted block after blighted block is anchored at each intersection with eight- to twelve-unit apartment buildings, many of which are vacant and boarded up or vandalized. Between these multi-story apartments on the corners of the blocks are two-flat townhouse structures with living units on each floor. Tackling the rehabilitation of the multi-story and multi-unit apartment buildings, which Uptown has tried, requires significant investment of staff, not only in family selection but also in homeowner association management. Working effectively in these blighted communities also requires significant interaction with existing neighborhood organizations and institutions.

From a construction and management point of view, a Habitat focus on the two-flat units would be more in keeping with our skill levels and volunteer capabilities. Such units offer the possibility of selling both to a single owner, who could then rent and manage the second unit, or selling both units to individual owners. In each case, we could minimize the challenges associated with homeowner associations. The larger apartment buildings should be targeted on a sparing basis and then only in partnership with other neighborhood associations and institutions that could participate in fund-raising and management.

Scheduling and planning this inner-city work on a blitz basis that incorporates several of the two-flat units creates a package that can attract both corporate funds and volunteers. Focusing this activity in a few selected neighborhoods could create synergy and partnerships with neighborhood organizations and be a catalyst for change and transformation.

In fact, the urban affiliate is faced with more limited resources than our suburban affiliates. The same volunteers who might gather in Du Page County, Illinois, and build four houses in three months are not likely to drive thirty or forty miles into the inner city and lend similar support weekend after weekend. Here again, the blitz approach offers the opportunity to fast-track our construction and to engage suburban churches and groups in a very focused and time-limited manner.

Is it possible to set up an Urban Habitat Association that would be responsible for fund-raising, public relations, and in-kind gifts? This association would request proposals from our urban affiliates that conform to the blitz approach and require the affiliates to demonstrate organizational ability, financial management and control, neighborhood participation, covenant compliance, etc. Grants would then be awarded on a competitive basis and be scheduled and coordinated to maximize Habitat's impact in that urban area.

This report raised issues that impacted most of our urban affiliates and began a dialog on affiliate mergers. Subsequently, several Chicago affiliates merged, and in November 2003, our board approved the merger of our inner-city Philadelphia affiliates. In 2005 the Los Angeles and Long Beach affiliates also merged. Hopefully this is the beginning of a rationalization of Habitat's organization in the United States that needs to continue. Currently there are three Habitat affiliates serving parts of Mecklenburg County, North Carolina. I know from experience that we trip over each other in fundraising and volunteer support. We could reap huge economies of scale in combing fund-raising and purchasing. We could trim costs by combining our mortgage servicing operations, and we could continue to organize family selection and construction on a community basis.

While nothing but their own inertia keeps these local affiliates from making such moves, there has been little support, challenge, or encouragement from Habitat for Humanity International staff, which until the last four months was still measured and weighed by its founding president based on the number of affiliates created each year. For Habitat to increase its effectiveness and house numbers in the United States, it must realign its affiliate program and pay more attention to merging and growing existing affiliates than creating new affiliates. This in fact was the focus of the 2005 reorganization of Habitat's operations in the U.S.

22

GROUNDED

One reason I left the ministry was because at the end of the day, I could see no measurable, quantifiable result. Yes, I spoke. But did anyone really listen? If they listened, did they understand? If they understood, did it make any difference in their lives?

One reason I really like Habitat for Humanity is because at the end of the day, a ditch has been dug, a footing poured, a wall built, or a door installed. And you can stand back and see it. And on those days when thirty or forty people gather to frame a house, you can stand back at dusk and see an entire house standing where only a foundation existed ten hours before.

Habitat for Humanity is grounded in stuff that is real, stuff you can see, touch, move, and erect. Yet long before that first ditch is dug, someone had to find, buy, and develop a lot for the house. Long before Mrs. Robertson's house was started, the volunteer members of Our Towns Habitat's board of directors located three acres on the south end of Meridian Street in Cornelius and raised $34,000 to purchase the property. This transaction occurred before I joined the Our Towns board. But when I joined the board, there was no development plan and no money in sight to pay for grading, storm drainage, water and sewer extensions, or street paving in the Meridian neighborhood.

For-profit home builders are always trying to balance and align three elements: customers, lots, and affordable loans. If loans are affordable, customers are plentiful and lots are often scarce. When interest rates rise, customers disappear and the home builder ends up with too many lots and too much inventory. Habitat affiliates struggle with aligning these same elements. Finding families who can qualify for even no-interest loans is a challenge. Assembling the volunteers to build those homes within a reasonable time requires skill and persistence. Securing lots and having them ready to meet the construction schedule may be the most difficult task of all. All of these efforts must be underwritten by consistent and effective fund-raising.

Centex challenged me. The day Centex closed on the purchase of Crosland, Harry Leonhardt, the CEO of Centex Homes, told me I would be successful with Centex if I got out from behind my desk. Harry believed in management by walking, driving, and flying around. In addition to overseeing home-building operations in North and South Carolina, Tennessee, and Virginia, Harry and his staff gave me the job of coordinating land development training for Centex divisions throughout the country. Joe Luciani, a very competent land development engineer, became my partner in this process.

Joe and I needed each other. Joe knew everything about land development and nothing about teaching. I knew a lot about teaching and nothing about land development. For seven years Joe and I traveled the country leading land development seminars we designed and wrote for Centex division personnel. Our seminars focused on case studies and site inspections as well as role playing. Land Development I presented the basic aspects of land planning, approvals, and construction supervision. Land Development II targeted not only division land development managers but also division presidents, controllers, and sales and construction managers. We devoted this seminar entirely to the issues involved in the fitting of a house to a lot, foundation height and cost, lot drainage, and customer expectations.

Land Development II began with a home video made by a Centex customer in Jacksonville, Florida. This customer was in her home when water began to rise in the street during a storm and entered her yard, threatening her house. It grabbed everybody's attention and was one of several customer stories that helped motivate the Centex division teams to improve their ability to site houses and control costs.

Because Centex divisions were located in forty markets in the United States, I was exposed to the land development challenges and issues in every region of the country, from the sandy soils of south Florida to the mountains of Tennessee, the plains of Texas, and the earthquake zones of California. I learned about impact fees designed to offset costs of new schools and fire stations, and efforts to control or slow growth. The regions where regulations made development more difficult and expensive proved a great advantage to companies such as Centex, which had the people and financial resources to meet these requirements. Limiting the supply of lots drives up the value of the lots approved for development and significantly increases the builder's margin.

I did not realize this at the time, but my land development assignment with Centex prepared me to contribute immediately to Our Towns Habitat. I knew what needed to be done with the Meridian Street property in Cornelius, who to call to get it done, and how to finance the development. Because I was serving on Habitat for Humanity's international Board at the same time, I also knew about land development grants Habitat International was administering for the Department of Housing and Urban Development, and that Our Towns Habitat could qualify for a grant for $7,500 per lot. Because I had worked with programs and staff from the Federal Housing Administration and the Department of Housing and Urban Development during my fourteen years with the John Crosland Company, I knew how to complete the forms and gather the information for timely project approvals.

So when Our Towns Habitat poured the footings for Patricia Robertson's house on Meridian Street, we were working on a lot I had helped finance, bid out, and develop along with nine other lots along Meridian Street and Fuller Street, a new street we named for Millard Fuller. Today ten Habitat families live in this neighborhood, supporting each other and the community they helped build. Meanwhile, I have used my knowledge and with the help of other board members assembled land in Mooresville, where we have built on five lots on Water Street; twelve lots in Thayer Court, a subdivision named for my mother's family; and thirty lots in Eddy Place, named for Henry Eddy, the father of Habitat in Mooresville and the man responsible for my love affair with Habitat.

Most Habitat affiliates in the United States and throughout the world do not know how to develop land. From its inception Habitat has been fortunate in many cities to be the beneficiary of vacant lots given by cities and towns in redeveloping neighborhoods. In 1999, as our international board began its strategic planning process, I called Tim Eller, Centex's president, to get his impressions of Centex's work with Habitat since 1992 and his recommendations of things Habitat needed to do differently in the future. This turned out to be a wake-up call for us.

Tim told me two things. First, he said that Habitat needed to invest more in staff and organization. His reports from Centex divisions working with Habitat affiliates across the country were mixed. Some Habitat affiliates obviously knew their work, were highly organized and worked efficiently with the Centex teams. Others were problematic. Tim mentioned that Habitat lacked consistency and needed standards and policies and trained people. By the way, Tim indicated that Centex was focusing internally on the same issues.

His second point was more telling. Tim asked, "Do you know those inner-city lots you guys have been getting for free or almost free?"

"Yes," I replied.

He said, "Because cities are now limiting suburban growth, Centex and other builders are coming back to the cities, and we are going to compete with Habitat for land and lots. Habitat needs a land strategy. Times have changed."

Seven years have passed since that conversation with Tim Eller. It would be fair to say that Habitat for Humanity International still does not have a land strategy. But we have talked about it. And we have some urban affiliates in Denver, Minneapolis, and Dallas that are becoming quite sophisticated in their approach to and knowledge of land development. Their strategies involve partnering with other organizations, such as housing authorities and builders, to be included in their developments. Habitat also has a land development handbook, compliments of Joe Luciani and Centex Homes, and our regional meetings include land development workshops. We have a long way to go, especially given the complexity of land issues around the world. In the United States alone, our Habitat affiliates are struggling to increase house production year after year, and land is at the center of this struggle.

Planes are grounded when unable to fly. A home builder without a steady and reliable supply of lots can be grounded in the same way. No lots, no homes. I am concerned that Habitat for Humanity is not yet sufficiently focused on land acquisition and development expertise and strategy to avoid a significant drop in U.S. house production before this decade passes.

23

HABITAT U.S.

At the conclusion of the Habitat for Humanity international board meeting in Chicago on October 19, 1996, Habitat had fifty-three pins in its world map marking countries where it had active programs. For all practical purposes Habitat started in Zaire about the same time it started in the United States. It was in Zaire that the Fullers, serving as missionaries for the United Church of Christ, began a housing program that became the forerunner of Habitat for Humanity. So from its inception, Habitat has been focused on worldwide housing needs, not just on needs in the United States.

In Habitat's earlier days, international partners and volunteers from the United States traveled to and lived in countries in Africa and Central America. There they established Habitat building programs embodying the principles of no interest, no profit, sweat equity, and Christ-centered love. Many of these projects flourished. Often Habitat homeowners and local families ran the programs under the direction of our international partners. In almost every case, the funding for these international projects came from Habitat for Humanity's fund-raising efforts in the United States. Since the international partners controlled the distribution of these funds, they also controlled the international projects.

In 1992, four years before I was elected to the board, the international board held a meeting in Uganda and passed what was called the

Entebbe Initiative. Prior to the meeting in Entebbe, Uganda, several board members traveled to Habitat projects in other African countries. What they learned there convinced them that Habitat projects in those countries should be governed and operated by each country's national residents, not by U.S. transplants or temporary volunteers. That was the purpose of the Entebbe Initiative: the end of U.S.-sponsored projects and the formation of national organizations to develop affiliates and provide oversight in each country.

During my first year on the board, I kept hearing about the Entebbe Initiative. Yet most often the mention of Entebbe was coupled with the plea for a national organization in the United States. If a national organization was good for Ghana or Guatemala, why wasn't it good for America? This question was being posed by a number of the U.S. citizens who were serving on the international board and who participated on the board's U.S. affiliate committee, which was powerless. The U.S. affiliate committee could hear complaints, propose policies, and make suggestions, but it was the international board that made all the decisions for Habitat U.S.

Without question, based on funds raised, numbers of affiliates, influence, and effectiveness, the Habitat for Humanity program in the United States was the reason Habitat could underwrite its operations in other countries. It seemed logical to me that Habitat in the United States needed its own national board and policies. But then I discovered that logic does not rule at Habitat. The logic of faith, perhaps, but not the logic of reason.

During my first few international board meetings, Habitat U.S. required 50 to 60 percent of the board's time. That time might have gone to the underfunded Urban Initiative, a failing affiliate such as the one in Chicago, or to Homestead, Florida. These affiliates struggled with building houses and managing funds, and they posed huge reputation risks for the entire organization. To save them, the organization often was faced with unplanned and unanticipated expenditures of capital and management time that significantly distracted it from international house building. To their credit, our international board members from Guatemala, Ghana, Australia, Netherlands, and the Philippines clearly saw what was happening. Yes, the United States was raising the bulk of the money, but it was also soaking up money and board time to the point that the other fifty-three countries with Habitat programs always appeared to come in second.

The more I listened, the more I began to understand why a U.S. national board might pose a problem for Habitat. The first issue was fund-raising. While U.S. affiliates raise their own program support from local donors and volunteers, Habitat for Humanity International over-lays these local fund-raising efforts with a direct marketing program that has sent up to forty million letters a year to prospective donors telling Habitat's story and soliciting contributions. The direct marking program accounts for 50 percent of Habitat for Humanity's gross income. It also is the source of most of the undesignated funds that are used to underwrite international house building. What might happen to this major fund-raising program if there were a U.S. national board? Who would control it? Would a U.S. board withdraw support from international house building, and could Habitat afford to take that risk?

But that was only one of the questions raised by the idea of a U.S. board and national organization. Who would be its president? If the president were not Millard, what would happen to Millard's power base and funding? If the president were Millard, what would happen to the international program; who would run it, and how would it raise money? Perhaps because of the difficulty of answering those questions, from 1996 to 2000 the wisdom of the international board had been to leave itself in charge of U.S. operations and to continue to call for the development of national boards and organizations outside the United States. But if one stays on a board long enough, there is a chance to participate in change. That happened to me.

Based on the bylaws in effect in 1999, I was not eligible for election to another term as an officer of the board. The new chair, Mick Kicklighter, appointed me as chair of the USA/Canada Subcommittee and chair of the Strategic Planning Committee. I also was serving on the Governance Task Force, through which the board in the late 1990s continued to wrestle with the governance issue of Habitat in the United States.

Many U.S. affiliates felt they had no voice in the way Habitat for Humanity conducted its business in the United States. Many of the larger and better-organized affiliates resented Habitat's direct-mail campaign and its many fund-raising intrusions into affiliate turf. Their calls to headquarters had gone unanswered so often they had quit calling. Through its Governance Task Force, the board developed the concept of creating a U.S. Council that would be comprised of six members of the international board appointed by the chair and nine members selected from Habitat's eight U.S. regions and its campus chapter program. The U.S. Council would have responsibility for guiding the U.S. program. The director of Habitat in the U.S. would work with and report to the U.S. Council. The council would approve the budget, formulate a strategic plan, devise policy, and communicate with U.S. affiliates.

When Mick Kicklighter appointed me as chair of the USA/Canada Subcommittee, he also asked me to organize and chair the U.S. Council. I consulted with my USA/Canada Subcommittee members and asked them to take on this dual role as well. In the spring of 2000, Habitat's U.S. staff provided names and résumés of people who might serve on the U.S. Council. The six international board members discussed the résumés and then conducted telephone interviews with twenty candidates for the nine positions. At the end of the process, we selected our nine representatives. I chaired the first meeting of the U.S. Council in Atlanta in May 2000.

We organized the council into three committees: Planning and Budget, Communications, and Policy and Governance. These committees, and especially the council members not drawn from the international board, energetically tackled their work. Standards of excellence for U.S. affiliates were reviewed, circulated for comment, approved, and properly communicated. A policy on collaborative fund-raising, over a year in process, gained acceptance both at international headquarters and among affiliates. Another policy on advocacy, giving advice and direction on political involvement, also was written, circulated, and approved. And most important, the international board reduced its time spent on U.S. issues to less than 5 percent. From the perspective of the international board, the U.S. Council pointed toward the possibility of other area councils and stronger governance at the area level.

Habitat for Humanity as an organization and a ministry is a work in process. This is especially true in the area of board governance and the need to move that governance closer to the people and communities served. The U.S. Council has become a laboratory for testing area governance and policy making at a level other than the international board. At my last board meeting in New Zealand, area subcommittees that oversee house-building programs throughout the world were raised to full committee status and empowered to add non-board members. This action fulfilled a goal I had as board chair for strengthening Habitat's work around the world. As a result of these changes, soon new ideas, energy, and enthusiasm will be coursing through Habitat's network, raising the effectiveness and profile of its work in every land.

24

BOARD WORK

It was customary for several spouses to attend the board meetings of Habitat for Humanity International. Usually they would come to breakfast, devotions, and dinner. Few attended our meetings. During the day they would explore the city hosting our meeting. In short order this group adopted a name: not "board spouses," but "bored spouses." We got the point and began to include activities for spouses wherever we went. The planned activities did not cause them to abandon their adopted name. They just used it less frequently.

When it comes to board work, I also often think "bored work," and boring meetings are fairly descriptive of the experience. This is true for many and maybe most organizations, but it is especially true for Habitat for Humanity. Compared to the excitement and joy of building, board work is pretty tame and time-consuming. Yet neither Habitat for Humanity International nor its affiliates could survive without it. It takes a committed and vibrant board to raise the funds, establish the policies, and employ the proper staff to guide and oversee Habitat's work. As is true for most nonprofit organizations, Habitat for Humanity board members volunteer their time and talent to support and guide its work.

A good example of the importance of board work, even when it is "bored work," is my experience with Our Towns Habitat. From 1995 to 2001 I served as president of the board of Our Towns Habitat and as a director on Habitat's international board. I wanted to do this because I felt that the knowledge I gained at the local level would guide me as I worked with my fellow directors to set overall policy and plans for Habitat for Humanity International.

Our Towns literally kept my feet on the ground. We were always running out of lots, and finding affordable land in a growing suburban area required significant attention. Jackie Hannon, a Habitat supporter and real estate agent, helped us look for land. Jackie and I would drive through Mooresville, Cornelius, and Huntersville looking for vacant property. Jackie would research and locate the property owner. We found a vacant four-acre tract in Mooresville that had three property owners. Our Towns did not have the money to purchase all the property at once, but to maximize its use, we needed to control all four acres. One owner agreed to a purchase and took a second mortgage for the property we would develop last. We proposed to another owner that we would pave a street into his property, increasing its value, if he would donate land for two lots to Our Towns. And the third owner gave the land to Habitat. Needless to say, this was a complicated transaction for what ultimately became a twelve-house community for Habitat. Considering the time that went into negotiating and preparing contracts, site plans, and development, Crosland or Centex would have produced two hundred lots.

But Our Towns not only ran out of lots; it ran out of space. Since its founding in 1989, the affiliate had leased warehouse space for a thrift store and a house for an office. In 1998 we heard from the property owners that our leases would be renewed only on a month-to-month basis. In other words, Our Towns Habitat was soon to be homeless. I got into my car and drove around again. I was looking for a place where our office and thrift store could be together. About that time, we learned that Grace Covenant Church, which had partnered with and built a house for a Habitat family, was going to move to a new location. The church building was located on Highway 115 in Cornelius. Highway 115 happened to be the main street in every town our affiliate served. And this church building included enough square footage to house our office and store. The church property consisted of the church building, a separate house used for church offices, a double-wide modular, and vacant property in the rear.

It was a big step for our affiliate to agree to pay $630,000 for anything, let alone an office building. But we knew how fast property values were rising and how fortunate we had been to lease property for so long. So we got creative. We agreed to purchase the property from Grace Covenant and then sell the house, which we did not need, and subdivide the vacant rear property into three lots for Habitat homes. The board approved, and late in 1999 the affiliate moved into its new home. The new location was so successful for the thrift store that in 2003 the affiliate rented a former grocery store next door to the office. Our Towns has now purchased this building.

Besides looking for lots and space, my fellow Our Towns directors and I looked for new board members. Our board consisted of twenty-one members. Each served a three-year term renewable for one term. We knew we needed people who could help raise money, guide construction, focus on our relationship with local churches, and assist in the family selection process. To this talent search we also had to add financial and public relations skills. These are the essential functions and responsibilities of an affiliate board.

Our board met monthly for two hours and gathered once a year for a strategic planning session that lasted four to six hours. Committee work required another two to three hours a month—unless you assisted in family selection, which required six hours or even much more in some months. Finding people who can and will commit this amount of time and energy to any organization is difficult. While the name of Habitat for Humanity is well known and respected, finding people today to serve on a local Habitat board is still a struggle, as the following story shows.

In January 2004, at Habitat's request, I visited and reported on an affiliate in Southern California. The affiliate had had eighteen houses under construction for two years, and not one was complete. Because of dwindling fund-raising and finances, the entire staff had been laid off fifteen months before my visit, and the board of directors had shrunk to five men who were meeting weekly to fend off creditors and figure out how to finish the project.

There is no way out of a problem like this that does not include finding new board members and revitalizing board committees so that the work of fund-raising, family selection, and building can continue. At almost every meeting of Habitat's international board, two or three local Habitat organizations are disaffiliated. Most often it is because the founding board members did not recruit their replacements, did not grow the board, and subsequently wore out.

At the beginning of 2005, there were about 1,670 and seventy Habitat affiliates in the United States. Every year almost 400 affiliates build no houses. Some affiliates are new and just getting organized. Some are in rural areas with highly limited resources. But most have not developed their board and the resources required to operate successfully.

Our Towns Habitat managed to strengthen its board with each new class of directors. We asked churches, donors, volunteers, elected officials, and professionals to recommend new board members. When we found a candidate, we would take time to meet with that person and explain carefully Habitat's work and purpose and also the kind of commitment we asked of board members. Many turned us down, and not all who said yes arrived with the needed time and energy. But we could always count on twelve to fifteen members of the board to attend meetings and lead committees carrying out the necessary board work. As a result, over a five-year period Our Towns Habitat increased its house construction from an average of four houses per year to nine per year, and through its store, mortgage repayments, grants, and fund-raising, Our Towns brought in close to a million dollars annually. Our Towns Habitat completed fifteen houses in 2005 and provided funding for another fifty international houses through its tithe to Habitat International.

Most important to me, when I left the Our Towns board my successor was in place and ready to assume the role of president. By all measures the affiliate has increased its strength, reputation, building sites and staff since my departure. There is no substitute at a local, national, or international level for effective governance, whether for Habitat for Humanity or any other business or organization, for-profit or nonprofit.

After my first year as chair of the international board, I had the responsibility to provide a performance review of Millard Fuller, Habitat's president and founder. I wanted to let Millard know that his fellow board members and I respected him and recognized and appreciated all of his work on behalf of Habitat and its mission, but also that he needed to acknowledge the importance of the board's role.

Millard has often referred to Habitat for Humanity as a movement, as in the coming of the kingdom of God on earth. Millard has told Christians everywhere that they do not have to worry about heaven. Jesus has taken care of that. Our job as Christians is to provide a simple, decent place to live for every family in need. Millard has tried to make the issue of simple, decent housing a matter of conscience, in the hope that people of goodwill around the world will join a housing movement.

So I suggested to Millard in December 2002 that movements by nature are chaotic. I told him that I knew he saw Habitat as a world movement and that his role was to create the excitement that got people's attention. Millard liked that idea. There is no better marketer in the world than Millard Fuller. Millard has more new ideas in a day than his staff could execute in a year. His zeal, energy, and new concepts kept people hopping, but they also kept the organization in frequent turmoil.

I then told Millard that the board's role, as I saw it, was to organize the excitement and chaos he engendered and to be sure that after he was no longer around there would be an organization capable of carrying on the work he had started. This thought commanded little attention from Millard. At sixty-seven years of age, he was thinking about living, not dying. Further, he argued that God would take care of Habitat's future. So he said, "You and the board do that—take care of the organization. I am going to continue to work on the movement, to push you and the staff and everyone else to build more houses, enter more countries, and raise more money to make it all possible." So despite the performance review and my best efforts to change Millard's attitude toward the board, it remained one of the matters over which he and I disagreed.

In response to Project Impact, the McKinsey report mentioned in chapter 21, Habitat began to move staff out of Americus and open area offices in places like San Jose, Costa Rica, and Bangkok, Thailand. The vice presidents running these offices took with them immense responsibility and assumed the authority to go with it. Before long, Habitat had lost $250,000 in a partnership with Shelter Afrique and an equivalent amount when a bank folded in Latin America. These events caused the international board to wonder who was watching the store. The board became concerned that we had decentralized our operations but not our governance.

The board chair, Mick Kicklighter, appointed a governance task force to examine the best way for a twenty-seven-member board that met two or three times a year to effectively oversee work in some seventy countries. I served on that task force. We thought our report was reasoned. We recommended that the area subcommittees, which were staffed by the vice presidents, should evolve over five years into area councils governing each area's work. We further recommended that membership on these councils should come from the national organizations in each area.

The program staff reacted immediately. Impossible, they said. We pointed out that the timetable was five years. Impossible, they said again. Through the discussions that followed, it became very clear that Habitat's approach to country development was to put a pin in the map, gather a few people who would take direction from our staff, and then fund construction. Little or no thought or effort went into building boards, developing organizational capacity, or conducting local fundraising. Consequently, when the international board began to consider representative area councils as an expanded form of governance, our staff had to admit that there were very few national board or committee members who were capable of serving on such a council.

In 1999, when I was asked to evaluate the Habitat program in India, I confirmed for myself the truth behind our staff's reaction to the area council proposal. During the thirty days I traveled in India, I met with the Habitat India national board of directors. At that time the entire board consisted of six directors, most of whom were pastors representing local affiliates. Their paramount interest in serving on that board was to gather as much of Habitat's funding for their own projects as possible. National staff paid by Habitat often worked at the affiliates that were fortunate enough to have a director on the national board. One staff member whose job description focused on new affiliate development was spending most of his time in Hyderabad, assisting with family selection for that affiliate. It just so happened that the president of that affiliate board also chaired the national board.

During my research, I found little evidence of a desire on the part of the national board to expand, to reach out to businesses and other institutions for funding, or to consider partnerships with Hindu or Muslim communities. Given the fact that Christians represented only 3 percent of India's population, I wondered how this board could ever develop a strong and vibrant national Habitat program.

When I was elected chair of the international board, my main focus was on strengthening our national organizations and developing forms of governance at every level capable of sustaining Habitat's work and of directing its program and staff. Chaos is good. Movements are powerful and compelling, but if that energy cannot be harnessed and directed, the movement is apt to die. Habitat for Humanity had a narrow window of opportunity while its founder was still alive and employed to strengthen its organizational capacity. The international board understood this opportunity and need. Habitat's founder wanted to add more pins to the map. I hope Habitat can figure out how to strengthen its existing national organizations and add new countries, but I would not sacrifice the strengthening and expansion of Habitat's existing operations in order to start work in a new country.

Using this approach Habitat can develop the capacity to build more houses and serve more families both now and in the future.

25

INNOVATION

The Merriam-Webster Online Dictionary defines *skunk works* as "a usually small and often isolated department or facility that functions with minimal supervision within a company or corporation." I cannot think of a better descriptive phrase to capture the essence and strength of Habitat for Humanity around the world: 100 countries, 2,400 affiliates, more than 800 campus chapters, and programs such as Building on Faith, Women's Build, Global Village, Operation Home Delivery, and so on. You name it—Habitat has it, or is in the process of creating it, complete with minimal supervision and thus an implied license for the program to wing it, figure out what works, and do its own thing.

For the most part, this mode of operating has served Habitat and its cause quite well. There have been tense moments when this loose organization has discovered some affiliates far afield, not collecting mortgage payments, failing to complete houses, not paying subcontractors, using balloon mortgages, diverting funds to building an office instead of building houses, or failing to meet the terms of government grants. Many of these discoveries have required the unplanned use of corporate funds and personnel to protect Habitat's name and reputation. But given the size of the organization, these misadventures so far have been relatively minor.

On the other side of the ledger, the relative freedom from interference enjoyed by Habitat partners has led to many innovative and creative approaches to fund-raising, family selection and support, house design, partnerships with other organizations, and governance. In fact, as Habitat looks to the future, it is focused on innovation as a key strategy to boost its house production and expand the pool of families it serves.

An artist in Jackson, Mississippi, designs and sells a new ceramic egg for Habitat every year, raising enough money in this single effort to build a house. The Lee County affiliate in Florida has acquired a lumberyard and panel shop, enabling the affiliate build one hundred houses per year. At almost every level, Habitat volunteers and staff are pushing the envelope.

While the international board has not been able to hammer out a policy and guide for interfaith cooperation, Habitat Jordan has arranged for its affiliate in Amman to have an all-Muslim committee. While Habitat registration in Egypt was delayed month after month, Habitat partnered with the Coptic Evangelical Organization for Social Service (CEOSS) to start building houses anyway, and together these organizations have created the most cost-effective and responsible Habitat program in all of Africa and the Middle East.

But I see the most dramatic potential in a relatively new house-building program created in Sri Lanka, out of the sight and reach of our Americus headquarters. There our Habitat families and staff asked themselves how they could serve their neighbors who could least afford a house. Their solution is called "building in stages." A stage-one house consists of one secure room with a floor and roof structure that supports the addition of rooms later. A family making less than a dollar a day can afford a stage-one house. But it was not enough just to create the concept, so a second notion was developed incorporating a micro-credit approach. Prospective Habitat families are now organized into groups of twelve, with each family contributing to the group's savings plan thirteen cents a day, the equivalent of one cigarette. At the end of six months, the families have saved enough for one family to start and pay for its stage-one house. At that point, Habitat matches the savings on a two-for-one basis so that three houses are started. Within two years all twelve families have a house, and within four years all the houses are mortgage free. What was launched as an experiment on the coffee plantations of Sri Lanka has now spread to Cambodia and Indonesia and soon will be working throughout our Asia Pacific region.

The power and the potential of building in stages, as well as the challenge to the typical approach of a Habitat affiliate, were demonstrated recently. Steve Weir, Habitat's vice president for Asia Pacific, was contacted by a women's microcredit organization in Nepal that had saved $5 million. They wanted to know if Habitat would help them build houses. Steve took this request to a Nepal affiliate. The affiliate committee had three questions: Who will build the houses? Answer: The women will. Who will select the families? Answer: All the women in this group meet Habitat's family selection criteria. They will decide who gets the houses. Who will handle the funds? Answer: The microcredit organization already has the funds.

Our affiliate turned down the request because it could not see a role for Habitat beyond its traditional roles of raising funds, selecting families, and building houses. What was needed here was simply a sharing of method and instruction to set the microcredit organization on its way to significant house building. Steve has not given up, and in the future Habitat might be less of a house builder and more of a teacher and organizer.

An offshoot of the building-in-stages approach has been a new program Habitat calls First Shelter. Habitat for Humanity has responded to several hurricanes and other natural disasters in Florida, Central America, and India. Typically we have sent out a mass mailing and direct appeal, often raising in excess of $1 million. But Habitat has used its traditional house-building method and thus has never really been among the first responders to such disasters. We have to organize an affiliate committee if one does not exist, and our potential homeowners must be able to repay the mortgages. The problem here is that in most of the areas impacted by hurricanes and earthquakes, the local economy is shut down for months and even years so that families have little or no income. In these situations Habitat's effectiveness and appeal have been eroded by programs that give away houses, such as those supported by the United States Agency for International Development (USAID).

First Shelter uses the concept of the stage-one house to interject Habitat as a first responder to disaster. All the Habitat principles, including sweat equity and partnership, apply to First Shelter, but the stage-one house is provided without a mortgage. Habitat works in the disaster area helping not only to build stage-one houses but also to organize an affiliate committee, teach building skills, and prepare for later stages of house construction, using our typical repayment method once the economy is restored.

Millard claimed that First Shelter is to our regular Habitat program as John the Baptist was to Jesus; that is, it is not Habitat, but it announces the coming of Habitat to people in distress. The First Shelter concept was tested during 2001 through 2003 in a partnership to build 579 houses with World Vision and USAID in response to the Gujarat, India, earthquake disaster.

It is this kind of innovation and openness to change that will be central to Habitat's future. It is anchored to Habitat's foundation as an entrepreneurial organization dependent on local communities and volunteers for its life and energy. The risks and downsides are the inefficiencies, for example, of five affiliates in Los Angeles County, California, all competing for the same funds while duplicating efforts, and the threat the failure of one of these entities holds for the other four. Habitat affiliates need to move from a competitive relationship to a cooperative relationship, eliminating needless duplication while doubling their efforts to innovate and reduce costs.

I am reminded of a weekend some time ago when I took my key John Crosland Company managers to Table Rock, North Carolina, for an Outward Bound adventure. We went to build teamwork and thought that the adventure of rock climbing and a ropes course would strengthen our work together. John Crosland Jr., the major stockholder and board chair, went with us. On the second night we camped in a clearing and were forewarned to tie up our food and garbage and hang it in the trees. Skunks had been spotted in this same location the night before. Well, the skunks returned about midnight, and in the moon's light I saw a skunk stop just to the left of my head and sniff. I did not move a muscle, and shortly he moved to the foot of my sleeping bag. Then he scrambled over to Crosland's sleeping bag. Then I was tempted to throw my shoe at the skunk and in an instant repay John for the daily grief he gave me. I resisted the temptation, and the skunk left without spraying John, but I reported to the group the next morning my missed opportunity. At that point, John said, "If you had done that, there would have been a change in command!" We all laughed.

I hope Habitat and its leaders will be successful in keeping its skunks from spraying and its skunk works creating the new programs and approaches essential for a vibrant future.

26

ADVOCACY

Habitat for Humanity International focuses on two goals. The first is to build as many houses as it can using the principles of sweat equity, no interest, no profit, and volunteer-driven construction—one house, one family at a time—in every corner of the world. Today Habitat for Humanity is completing a house somewhere in the world every twenty-four minutes, or twenty thousand houses per year. This record is impressive in some ways, especially when viewed through the eyes and experiences of homeowners and volunteers. But compared to the housing needs in this world, it is not much bigger than a flea on the back of an elephant.

This is where Habitat's second goal comes in. We are going to make housing a matter of conscience everywhere, every day, every moment, for every person we meet. Habitat wants everyone to understand that it is morally and socially unacceptable for any human being—child, parent, young, old, or in between—not to have a simple, decent place to sleep at night. When enough folks get this message, people will change the conditions of hopelessness and despair created by the lack of a simple, decent home.

Habitat for Humanity calls this second goal advocacy, and it challenges its affiliates and partners everywhere to ask these questions:

- Is your Habitat affiliate recognized as a turn-to "voice" on the issues of adequate shelter in your community?
- Have you developed effective advocates—writers, speakers, and so on?
- Do you have the information to effectively discuss the state of housing in your service area?
- Do you participate in meetings and conferences on the needs of families for adequate shelter?

What these questions drive home is Habitat's inability to solve housing issues alone. Our Denver, Colorado, affiliate recently spoke out when a state-wide proposition called for restricting new housing developments to large lots. This proposition's passage would have been a disaster for low-income housing. Until Habitat representatives spoke up, voters were inclined to pass the amendment. But because of the Denver affiliate's intervention, the proposition was defeated. Subsequently, Habitat's U.S. Council developed a policy on advocacy that spells out the prohibitions that 501(c)(3) corporations face in regard to electioneering, but at the same time clarifies the right to educate the public and to speak out on issues of affordable housing. For Habitat to make housing a matter of conscience in this country and throughout the world, its supporters must speak out.

In my role as board chair, I had several opportunities to speak, and one of those was at the Washington State Affordable Housing Conference in Seattle on October 30, 2002. The conference's theme was "With a Little Help from Our Friends," and it focused on the various accomplishments of housing groups in Washington State, made possible in part by the support received from the Washington State Housing Finance Agency. Judy and I both looked forward to this conference, partly because of the conference itself and partly because it meant we could spend a few days with our grandchildren who live in Everett, Washington.

Judy's father traveled with us, and for several days before my speaking engagement, we played with Ian and Sam, our grandsons, and took Judy's father on several sightseeing trips around Seattle. I woke up on the Sunday morning prior to Wednesday's scheduled speech with a new and very noticeable pain in my right side. Judy, known to friends and family alike as "Nurse Leonard" because of her nursing skill, degrees, and experience, immediately diagnosed possible appendicitis. I, on the other hand, immediately thought Judy had assumed the worst of all scenarios, so I took a hot bath and went back to bed. The pain intensified, and at 11:00 a.m. we arrived at the Everett Medical Clinic. By 6:00 p.m. my appendix had been removed. Nurse Leonard was basking in her diagnostic ability, and Patient Paul was wondering what had hit him.

Because of the miracles of modern medicine, by 11:00 p.m. I was gingerly walking in the hall near my hospital room trying to encourage my bodily functions to resume so that I could be discharged from the hospital the next morning. I also was wondering about Wednesday night's speech and, beyond that, Thursday's flight back to Charlotte followed by Sunday's Dream Dinner speech for Our Towns Habitat and the following Monday's flight to Belfast. Monday morning, no doctor. Monday afternoon, no doctor. Early Monday evening, finally, a doctor gave me permission to leave. By that time, I was too tired to leave. Indigestion was killing me, and I just wanted to be left alone. Enter Nurse Leonard.

"I am taking you home. Get dressed while I go for the car."

"Yes, dear!"

She was right again, but I did surprise her when I walked out of the hospital on my own. Transportation, meaning a wheelchair, took forever, and finally I had told the floor nurse I was leaving, stepped into the elevator, and went to find Judy.

The doctor had said that I could speak Wednesday night but should limit my lifting and walking for a few days. Nurse Leonard rounded up a wheelchair and paid me back for the rides I gave her when her ankle was broken. It was a long push from our hotel room to the conference room on Wednesday evening, but we made it. By Wednesday, the pain from the surgery had subsided, and as long as I did not lift anything, I experienced little pain. After they played the Habitat video I had brought, I rose from the wheelchair, walked up the steps to the podium, and laid it on for advocacy and for Habitat. Here is some of what I said:

My Habitat for Humanity friends think I have gone off the deep end! "Why," they ask, "do you want to show a ten-year-old video to introduce Habitat?"

I could tell them, "Some things never change. The housing problems of ten years ago are still with us." Or how about this: the goal of the 1949 Housing Act, fifty-three years ago, of "a decent home and affordable living environment for every American" is still not realized. While these are both true statements, they are not the reasons you saw this video. There are two reasons. The first is personal.

In 1992 the Jimmy Carter Habitat project in Washington, D.C., opened my eyes. I was there to work on the Centex Homes house. I knew something about affordable housing before arriving in D.C. Over a long home-building career, I had developed affordable single-family subdivisions under the FHA Section 235 program. I had developed and syndicated a number of apartment communities in two states under both Section 236 and Section 8 programs. I had assembled and rehabilitated properties with over two thousand apartments though city- and state-issued revenue bonds.

Here is what I did not know. I did not know the impact a simple, decent, secure place to live has on a family. I did not realize the hope and promise it gives to children. I had not seen the stress and agony decent housing lifts from the shoulders of parents. I did not appreciate the strength decent housing lends to a community. I did not realize that working with a family and other volunteers could change my life, lift my spirit, bring tears to my eyes, fill me with a deep sense of satisfaction and gratitude, and make me want to do this over and over again.

Here is the other reason you saw this video. I wanted everyone here tonight to remember why you work for affordable housing. I wanted to remind you that it is not the grants from the Housing Trust Fund or the allocation of federal tax credits or the sites you optioned or the plans you drew or the houses you built that are ultimately important. It is the adults, children, and families you helped. Look into the eyes of a Pam Bundy [in the video], listen to her voice, hear her husband whisper, "It's a miracle," and then tell me you are not in the business of changing lives, building hope, and transforming communities.

Our housing approaches differ. Habitat for Humanity is a home-building company of volunteers that seeks donated funds from individuals, businesses, churches, and government, which are then recycled through no-interest, no-profit twenty-year mortgages. The Washington State Housing Finance Commission uses a variety of programs to promote development of rental and for-sale housing and to educate housing consumers, and from its inception in 1983 has participated in the development of thirty-one thousand homes, forty-eight thousand apartments.

But no matter what approach we use, we are all inseparably linked together in this effort to ensure that everyone in the state of Washington has a simple, decent place to live. In the 1960s we might have called our efforts a war on poverty housing. Today, there is no housing war, no clamor, no movement, no notice, no recognition of the vitally important, life-sustaining, hope-giving, community-building power that affordable housing brings to a community and a state.

The issue of affordable housing has lost favor. David Broder, who writes for the *Washington Post*, pointed out recently that, except for a few cities, housing is the forgotten issue. Broder also observed that the report of the Millennial Housing Commission mandated by Congress landed this May in Washington with a thud after seventeen months of work. Boston mayor Thomas Menino, president of the U.S. Conference of Mayors, said recently that the nation's affordable housing crisis should be on everyone's radar screen right now, but it is not. Why is there no Homes across America program today as there was in 1992 when I went to D.C.?

Some suggest that it is because housing has been a great American success story. We sometimes lose perspective. Eighty-eight years ago the average down payment on a house equaled two-thirds of the purchase price, and the mortgage was six to eleven years. Seventy-three years ago the required down payment had decreased to 50 percent of the purchase price and 48 percent of American families owned a home. That was until the 1930s when there were one thousand foreclosures per day and over 50 percent of homeowners were in default. The rise in the percentage of Americans owning homes has been dramatic, from 48 percent in 1929 to 67 percent today, but there have also been periods of setback and decline because of inflation, recessions, and increasing divorce rates. We also know home ownership rates are not the same for all classes of American citizens or for all states. In this state only 64.6 percent of its housing is owner-occupied, according to the 2000 census. Still, the American housing story is one of unparalleled success in the world.

But past success in this state and in our nation is no reason to ignore and turn away from America's current housing crisis and the families struggling to make ends meet. It has been twelve years since Congress passed a comprehensive housing bill. Nationwide, 28 million families, 25 percent of all families, spend more on housing than the 30 percent of their income the federal government considers affordable. In Washington State alone, more than 4000,000 low-income households spend more than 30 percent of their income on housing. Nationally, one in eight low-income families, working for minimum wage, spends more than 50 percent of their income for housing.

The National Housing Conference warns that unless something is done and soon, more police, firefighters, school teachers, nurses, sales clerks, and their families will join the millions who already can't afford to live in their communities. Public housing is in decline in almost every city due to limited maintenance funds. This fact is not likely to change. In a 2003 interview, Department of Housing and Urban Development Secretary Mel Martinez said that "housing issues are predominately local issues. The solution to meeting the nation's affordable housing needs will not come out of Washington." Thank you very much, Mr. Secretary. We sensed this to be true. Now you have confirmed it.

In other words, the housing ball is in our court, yours and mine. It belongs to the State of Washington, to the counties, cities, towns of America—and to the agencies, organizations, and businesses represented here tonight. The housing ball is in our court. If we cannot declare war, then let's declare outrage; let's let everyone in this state know that it is morally and socially unacceptable for its citizens to live in overpriced, unsafe, dilapidated houses and apartments or to sleep under I-5 overpasses or in downtown doorways.

Let's tell the story in the ways folks can get it. We often fret about high land cost and unwelcoming neighborhoods. We focus on tax credits and design standards. We worry about equitable distribution formulas funding housing in urban and rural settings. And these concerns are all important, but they are not our story.

Our story is the Pam Bundys of this country. Our story is Laurel Devakenner and daughters, Shalicia, two, and Patricia, five, who spent five months in a Snohomish County homeless shelter in search of a more permanent home they could afford. Our story is Angela Bradford and six-year-old Michael and six-month-old De Andre who, thanks to Seattle's Mutual Interest Program, could move from temporary to more permanent housing.

These are the stories we must tell, and there are hundreds of thousands of them in the state of Washington alone. According to last year's report prepared for the Washington State Housing Finance Commission by the Washington Center for Real Estate Research, 195,751 households making 50 percent or below of median income lack affordable places to live. This does not even address the crowd whose income exceeds 50 percent of median and who are also struggling. . . .

Millard Fuller, Habitat's founder, often told us, "We have the know-how to house everyone in the world." We have the resources to house everyone. All that is missing is the will to do it. So you will find in many communities where Habitat works today that we are talking about the 21st Century Challenge. We are organizing communities and challenging them to set a realistic date, no more than twenty years away, to eliminate substandard, overcrowded, unaffordable housing conditions in their communities, to reach out to neighborhood residents and develop community coalitions to rid our country of this blight, and our children and families of this burden. Decent, affordable housing should not be a lottery for a few lucky families. In the most prosperous nation in the history of the world, decent and affordable housing must be a basic human right.

On its website, the Washington State Housing Finance Commission declares that its mission is to increase housing access and affordability. Let's do more than increase housing access. Let's put an end to poverty housing and set a date by which it would be accomplished. Forty communities in the United States have embraced the 21st Century Challenge and are developing the coalitions that will ensure that every family in their borders has a simple, decent place to live. Ten of these communities have set dates. . . .

I appreciate the theme of this conference: "With a Little Help from Our Friends." I celebrate with you the recognition these friends of housing so richly deserve. But surely this is a subtle understatement. With a little help from our friends, we will get little accomplished. We need a larger vision. Let's put an end to the misery and burdens that homelessness and unavailable, unaffordable housing create. We need a lot more friends and a lot more help, and it is not coming from our nation's capital and maybe not from Olympia either.

I know the record of your accomplishments. I know what this group can accomplish. Here's my challenge: Set the dates, disturb the complacent, and tell the stories that can put Washington State in the vanguard of communities that make decent and affordable housing the cornerstone of its common society. Together we can do more than increase access to affordable housing. We can eliminate the problem.

Let me close with this story. A man fell over the edge of a steep cliff. He could have been on Mount Rainier or Mount Baker. As he hurtled through the air, he reached out and grabbed hold of a root growing out from the wall of the cliff. Gripping that root for dear life, he shouted up to the top of the cliff. "Help! Is anybody up there?" To his utter surprise, a voice answered. "Let go of the root," it said. "I am God, and if you let go of the root, I will catch you and bring you up safely." The man paused and then shouted, "Is there anybody else up there?"

That is what the Pam Bundys of this world and of this state want to know as they cling to the roots of their lives: "Is there anybody else up there?" What will you tell them?

When I finished my talk and took my seat, the president of the Washington State Housing Finance Agency thanked me and noted that I, in my post-op wheelchair, had set a new standard. No longer would the agency accept colds and sore throats as a reason not to come to work. I hope I also raised their standards and goals for producing affordable housing. I have lived long enough to know that if we do not engage in the political and legislative processes at every level of government, the needs of housing will always take a backseat to those who speak and squeak the loudest.

27

CAPACITY

I believe Habitat's international board chose the right word to describe one of its goals for the organization's future. There was clear vision about building one hundred thousand houses and operating in one hundred countries in five years. Accompanying that vision was a strong sense that Habitat needed to build capacity not only for the next one hundred thousand houses and one hundred countries but also for a future extending well into the twenty-first century. And everywhere we turned, capacity was lacking—in resource development, in staff, in national organizations and in both internal and external communications.

Recently I was stopped at a roadside license check, and the first thing the officer noted was that my inspection sticker was eight months out of date. No excuse. I had been so busy tending to family, to business, to Habitat that I had neglected my main means of transportation. The officer was right. Fortunately for me, he gave me a note of caution and not a ticket, and I gave him my promise to get the car inspected before the week had ended. When I took my car in, it needed a new set of tires before it would pass inspection, and a wheel alignment to go with it. Focused on other concerns, I had ignored my car's tires and its ability to steer and stop within proper limits. In some ways, this is a metaphor for how Habitat's international board saw the organization: overextended, worn out, and neglected. Maybe we would build that next one hundred thousand houses or drive another one hundred thousand miles, but unless we did something to build up the capacity of the organization, it could well be the last one hundred thousand we would build.

As I mentioned in chapter 2 when Centex Real Estate Corporation purchased John Crosland Company in 1987, the Centex executives made it clear that they had only two interests: people and land. People and land are the critical assets of any home-building company, and since the John Crosland Company had an ample supply of land and many talented and capable employees, Centex made the deal and paid a premium for the company.

What are the critical assets of Habitat for Humanity, beyond the obvious asset of our founder, with his energy and vision? What might happen when Millard Fuller was no longer on the scene, and when would that be? Will Habitat have put in place an organization capable of carrying on its work around the world? Will we have the people who can persevere, raise funds, tell the story, build excitement, and grow the productive capacity of the organization? The responsibility for answering these questions fell squarely on the shoulders of the international board of directors, and from there to the shoulders of senior staff and to the boards of all our national and local affiliates. After January 31, 2005, with Millard's termination everyone had to take on the challenge of Habitat's future.

The international board has asked all its affiliate boards and staffs some key questions: What are your building targets, and what would they be if you really stretched? How will you raise money to meet those targets? How will you acquire the land upon which to build? Do you have the proper staff and volunteer base to meet the building targets? Does your staff and volunteer base reflect the demographics of your service area? Are staff and volunteers compensated and recognized appropriately? Are you meeting the tithe expectation by sending 10 percent of your nondesignated funds to Habitat's international work?

These are serious questions, most of which, if the Habitat family is honest with itself, would have to be answered in the negative. Previously I mentioned the southern California affiliate that could not complete construction on eighteen homes. That affiliate had dismissed its entire staff and struggled to pay its creditors. Funds secured from Los Angeles County and the State of California had been spent, and efforts at local fund-raising were almost nonexistent. This was a classic case of chasing a worthy vision and ignoring capacity. Fourteen of the homeowners originally approved for the eighteen houses were still hanging on. One family had been approved more than four years ago and had invested over one thousand hours of sweat equity and was still waiting for the promised house. An article in the *Los Angeles Times* had carried the headline "Habitat Needs a Miracle." It was not a miracle the affiliate needed, but a competent board and staff capable of raising money and matching resources to plans. I can report today that this affiliate has recruited new board members, raised funds, hired new staff and completed most of the houses. The experience of this affiliate is for me a microcosm of the larger issues faced by Habitat International as it pursues a wonderful and moving vision without putting an equal emphasis on its human and financial capacity.

Here is another example that illustrates for me the consequences of inattention to sound management principles and practices. I don't know the other side of this story. I have not spoken to the affiliate. But I do know John. John retired from a successful career with General Motors and then worked as a construction manager for a local Habitat affiliate. The agreement with Habitat was for thirty to thirty-five hours per week. John worked sixty hours many weeks, and with the help of his brother, Ed, a retired GM supervisor, and other volunteers they built five houses a year. For some reason, the Habitat board was not happy with John. They wanted to dictate the hours, times, and places he worked. Increased tension and conflict led to a final meeting in which the board president, who had never worked on a Habitat house, told John, "You work for us, and if we tell you to go to an empty lot and pick up dead cats, that's what you will do." John did not pick up dead cats. He picked up his Day-Timer and left his job with that affiliate. Ed left with John, and perhaps other volunteers left as well. House building declined from five to three per year. As I said, I don't know the other side of this story. I do know that John and Ed are still working at a number of different affiliates. I also know this is not the way Habitat is supposed to work.

Our call is to demonstrate the love of God in caring for and building houses with people in need. Along the way, we need to demonstrate that same care and love for those who work beside us. It is this love in action, coupled with no interest and no profit, that distinguishes Habitat for Humanity from all other home-building ventures. Each affiliate and every arm of Habitat would do well to look in the mirror and be sure it is reflecting on the inside what it purports to represent on the outside. If there are any dead cats, I suggest we remove them together and recommit to the principles, spirit, and love that drive this work.

Taking care of your people includes paying them a reasonable wage and not trading on their faith commitment to cut a better deal for the organization. It has taken the full attention and pressure of the international board to raise salaries and benefits for the employees of Habitat International and to put in place a compensation system with compensation scales and job descriptions and classifications. Yet under Millard's watch hardly a meeting went by during which our president and founder didn't complain that even with the higher salaries encouraged by the board, Habitat was not producing more houses. It would be nice if cause-and-effect relationships were so direct that a $2-per-hour increase in salary would build five more houses. But Habitat does not work that way, and neither does any other organization.

There is, however, a direct relationship between our capacity to build houses overseas and the tithe paid by United States affiliates to support this work. The affiliate covenant calls for each affiliate to tithe 10 percent of its undesignated income, excluding gifts in kind, to Habitat's work in other countries. In 2004 U.S. affiliates tithed over $10 million to our international work, which amounted to only 3 percent of more than $300 million of estimated unrestricted income. The truth is that for the average cost of every house built in the United States, Habitat could build fourteen houses almost anywhere else in the world. If Habitat had received a full tithe from its U.S. affiliates, worldwide housing production last year would have increased by almost five thousand houses, or 25 percent. This is one reason Judy and I agreed, starting in the December 2003, to co-chair the House for House Campaign, which encourages U.S. affiliates to increase their average tithe from $2,000 per house built in this country to $4,200. This amount still falls short of a full tithe, but it is one step that can strengthen the overseas work and increase our capacity in areas of the world's greatest housing need.

Another area in which we are trying to build capacity is resource development. From its inception Habitat has relied heavily on direct mail to raise undesignated funds to support both its headquarters staff and its international work. A few years ago Habitat was mailing forty million letters a year and generating a 1 percent response with an average gift of $25. This response paid for the cost of the initial mailing and in subsequent letters to the respondents, 34 percent would become regular donors to Habitat's work. The cost of raising money this way was 50 cents on the dollar. In the last few years, the cost of the mailings has increased and the response rates have dropped, making direct mail an even less favorable way to raise funds.

Habitat has launched what I think could become a more promising approach to its fund-raising. There are now thirteen major gift officers spread throughout cities in the United States. These gift officers call on donors who, over their lifetime, have given at least $5,000 to Habitat for Humanity. The donors are thanked personally and given the opportunity to commit funds at even higher levels. As board chair, I made donor calls with gift officers in Seattle, Orlando, Tampa, Sarasota, Charlotte, and Boston. Often I would begin a conversation with a donor by asking how he or she first got involved with Habitat. I was struck by the fact that several donors did not remember and could not answer my question. A few said, "Well, I saw Jimmy Carter on television." These responses told me two things. First, I needed to stop asking that question, because direct-mail donors were likely to realize they had no real connection to Habitat—and if they had no real connection, they weren't apt to step up for huge increases in their giving. And second, I needed to consider all the volunteers working at our affiliates with our U.S. homeowner families or traveling abroad with Habitat's Global Village Work Teams, who can tell you the moment their hearts were moved by this work and who seldom have been asked for a major gift. It is the affiliates that have the most committed workers and best donor prospects, and it is the international staff that has the professional ability to ask for significant gifts. So my theme song for our resource development team was collaboration. Figure out how you can work with the affiliates. Find a way to share the gifts that increase the bottom line for our work at both the local and the international levels.

This collaborative approach got lip service but not much else. International is afraid to take the risk of working closely with the affiliates, afraid the affiliates will end up with most of the gifts. I know it is lip service because major gift officers get zero credit for any gifts they raise for affiliates, even when their efforts raise hundreds of thousands of dollars. They also get zero credit for multi-year pledges. In other words, bring the cash to Habitat for Humanity International today and you will be rewarded; nothing else matters. It is a sure formula for failure, and it undercuts the ability of Habitat International to gain creditability with the U.S. affiliates that need the professionalism and experience the international staff could bring to them. Thankfully, when we hired a new senior vice president of resource development in January 2005, we began to change this approach and both raise the importance and re-cognition of collaborative fundraising.

Maybe I just couldn't see it from where I sat. Maybe Millard knew better than I did why it had to be this way. But I was not convinced, and given the high turnover rates and falling morale among the major gift officers, I suspected Millard was looking back to the way things were instead of forward to the dawning of a new day for Habitat, which his own preaching had brought to pass. Habitat's future de-pends on the relatively untouched capacity of affiliate donors, and most affiliates need Habitat International's ability to raise funds if that donor capacity is going to be harnessed for this work. We cannot fight turf wars over donors' gifts and expect to reach higher levels of house production.

True capacity building within Habitat will require genuine coopera-tion and must be based on mutual trust, not lip service.

28

BEYOND HOUSES

A report in the first-quarter 2004 issue of *The Affiliate Update*, published by Habitat for Humanity International, focuses on the importance of homeownership. Maureen Crawford, vice president of affiliate services for Habitat Canada, reported that in a survey of Habitat families in Canada, respondents cited feelings of financial security and tenure as the most important benefits of owning their homes. Not far behind in importance was improvement in children's grades, due either to being in a better neighborhood and school district or to having improved health and ability to concentrate. Additionally, children were found to be happier, more outgoing, and more confident. Parents thought this was because a child had a room of his or her own, and there was more room in the house in general. In almost a fourth of the houses, one or both spouses had returned to school or upgraded their job skills. Soon Habitat will have even more information on homeownership, because Habitat International has commissioned Dr. Don Haurin, an economics professor at Ohio State University, to develop a standardized survey all affiliates can use to test the impact of homeownership among Habitat families.

This report from Canada is great news, and it is consistent with the firsthand evidence I have seen among Habitat families I know and have worked beside. Yet these additional benefits accruing from homeownership are almost an indirect consequence of homeownership. They were not something Habitat planned; they just turned out to be significant by-products of the home-building process.

I am looking for something more, something beyond houses that is intentional and deliberate, planned from the beginning and part of Habitat's impact on both families and communities. From my very first board meeting in Manila, where I saw raw waste flowing beside the streets in a new Habitat community, I thought Habitat needed to broaden its focus and, by working in partnership with other groups and agencies, provide potable water, improve sanitation, develop schools, ensure medical care, and improve income opportunities. I was pleased in Baanuase, Ghana, to see a teak forest that had been planted by the homeowners and would be harvested by them one day for the benefit of their community. I was not pleased that the women in this community had to walk a mile for water and that streets were graded with no thought to storm water runoff.

I also was not pleased when Millard questioned why my friends on the A-Team had partnered with these homeowners to build an elementary school in that community. Millard said that Habitat builds the houses, and those in the community can take care of the rest. But I am not so sure. After all, how hard would it be to get World Vision or CARE or some other agency to partner with us to develop more livable and sustainable communities? I was pleased at the Trichy affiliate in India to discover that homeowners were provided with a buffalo for milk and income. I am not pleased to know that little thought is given to income generation among Habitat's worldwide operations.

But it was through Habitat international that I met Keith Jaspers in 1995, just after Keith had founded the Rainbow Network, a nonprofit organization that specializes in long-term, partnership-based community development programs in Nicaragua. Judy and I met Keith in Americus at a Presidential Weekend for donors. Keith had formerly served on Habitat's international board. He supported Habitat, but he was even more excited about his vision for Nicaragua, the second-poorest nation in our hemisphere. Keith and his wife, Karen, owned a hotel franchise in Branson, Missouri, about the time Branson became a hot tourist destination. His success in business had enabled him and Karen to establish a private foundation to underwrite the work in Nicaragua.

At first it sounded as if Keith was following the Habitat model and just building homes. But as he talked, the vision grew to include medical and dental teams, supplemental after-school programs for elementary school children, scholarships for high school students, and microcredit loans for family businesses. Judy and I were moved by Keith's vision and holistic approach to community development, and from that day we have supported the Rainbow Network (www.rainbownetwork.org).

Fast-forward from 1995 to 2005, and you will find the Rainbow Network in Nicaragua in six city areas (networks) covering about 1,800 square miles and serving more than 44,000 people. Each network employs six full-time professionals, educated in Nicaragua and focused on health care—including medical, dental, and optical programs—education, economic development, and housing. Two hundred fifty houses are under construction, built with volunteer labor and materials provided by Rainbow Network donors. The mortgages will have no interest charges and be repaid in ten to twenty years, depending on a family's income. One thousand microcredit loans of up to $150 per family are being repaid with interest from family businesses.

Hundreds of high school students from the poorest villages are attending high schools with the support of donors who pay $22 per month to sponsor and become acquainted with a student. Teeth are filled for 65 cents per filling, and eye exams and prescription glasses are available for under $12, with loans for those who cannot pay up front. Certainly by American standards these charges seem more than reasonable, but an average family in the rural area of Nicaragua earns only the equivalent of about U.S. $500 per year.

The Rainbow Network, like Habitat, is a Christian ministry dedicated to sharing Jesus' love. I am not close enough to this work to understand if this love is totally free and requires no conversion or prayer or church attendance. But knowing Keith, I feel certain it is. And it seems to me that Keith and the Rainbow Network have found an effective way to look beyond houses and address the most basic needs of a poor community. I was excited to read in Keith's latest letter that the Rainbow Network and Habitat are partnering to build houses in one of the networks' communities. This is exactly the type of partnership Habitat needs to join and/or create if it is to build sustainable communities and improve not just the houses but the overall living conditions of its families.

Habitat's Save and Build program in Southeast Asia takes a step in this same direction, using microcredit principles to save for housing. But Habitat's overall track record for community development comes up short. For too long we have tried to do it alone, played our game, and ignored some of the larger issues struggling families face. Maybe the challenge we should undertake in the twenty-first century is not the elimination of poverty housing community by community, but the elimination of poverty with all its numbing and killing effects.

Habitat must invite other organizations to play a role and bring their ability to drill wells, make loans, and attend to health. Habitat must be intentional about working holistically and no longer leave the future of our Habitat families and communities to chance. If Habitat is going to make housing a matter of conscience, let it also make the conditions that surround poor and desperate communities a matter of conscience. Let Habitat lend its voice to others who advocate for the education and employment that are essential for sustainable communities. Let Habitat become an active partner in the larger network of organizations and agencies focused on the needs of the poor. Let Habitat reach beyond houses.

Index